POETRY MATTERS

Edited by Claire Tupholme

North & East Yorkshire

First published in Great Britain in 2011 by:

YoungWriters

Remus House
Coltsfoot Drive
Peterborough
PE2 9BF
Telephone: 01733 890066
Website: www.youngwriters.co.uk

Book Design by Samantha Wood

SB ISBN 978-0-85739-303-6

Foreword

Since our inception in 1991, Young Writers has endeavoured to promote poetry and creative writing within schools by running annual nationwide competitions. These competitions are designed to develop and nurture the burgeoning creativity of the next generation, and give them valuable confidence in their own abilities.

This regional anthology is one of the series produced by our latest secondary school competition, *Poetry Matters*. Using poetry as their tool, the young writers were given the opportunity to tell the world what matters to them. The authors of our favourite three poems were also given the chance to appear on the front cover of their region's collection.

Whilst skilfully conveying their opinions through poetry, the writers showcased in this collection have simultaneously managed to give poetry a breath of fresh air, brought it to life and made it relevant to them. Using a variety of themes and styles, our featured poets leave a lasting impression of their inner thoughts and feelings, making this anthology a rare insight into the next generation.

Contents

Ripon College, Ripon

The Poems

We Are Paramore

To write something I'm passionate about,
A harder task than first thought.
Something I could powerfully shout about.
But my mind is caught.

Because there is one thing in my life,
And one thing only,
That throws away all grief,
That makes me feel less lonely.

From the first day I heard the almighty riffs of Misery Business,
And heard the pint-sized flame of girl sing,
I could tell, this band was ageless
Even if the group were just a fledgling.

Every tour I find myself standing in a pit.
In a sea of others just like me,
Girls with red hair, the same outfit
When the intro kicks in, we scream back the melody.

The Only Exceptions, that's what they are.
Hayley, Taylor, Zac, Josh and Jeremy
Misguided Ghosts that have come so far.
Pushed themselves past the limit and eventually became enemies.

Through Brand New Eyes they realised
After a Riot! broke out,
That all they know is falling, their friendship had capsized,
Took the backwards race and found the right route.

The quintet from Franklin standing, once again,
God knows the world doesn't need another band,
But millions waiting for the Miracle, said amen.
And they came back fighting as if it all had been planned.

You see music isn't an obsession.
It's released. As escape.
Part of the soul, the body, a working organ,
The silver glint of hope when your world is misshaped.

Jemma Watling (14)
Barlby High School, Barlby

Who's That Girl?

Who's that girl?
With jet black hair and skin as white as winter snow,

Who's that girl?
With the darkest of brown eyes and lips as red as rubies,

Who's that girl?
Listening to eighties music and eating expensive prime fillet steak,

Who's that girl?
Who always has to sit by the window to see the world and cringes when her feet rub on the carpet,

Who's that girl?
Who reads romantic novels like 'Where Rainbows End' over and over again, and can suck on 'Rowntrees' pastels without chewing,

Who's that girl?
Who loves to leap and dive in the snow and can't whistle to save her life,

Who's that girl?
Who hates the smell of newspaper but loves going on long strolls down the cycle track with her best friends,

Who's that girl?
Who took keyboard lessons and could ride roller coaster rides for a living,

Who's that girl?
Who enjoys watching gory movies with the family and can't keep a pair of shoes without breaking them shortly after buying them,

Who's that girl?
Who doesn't mind getting lost and is willing to buy a broken bag for forty pounds,

Who's that girl?
Who thinks elephants are the most adorable creatures and when she was younger she wanted to be a mermaid, she still wants to be a mermaid,

Who's that girl?
With a wobbly front tooth and believes 3 is her lucky number because when you turn it round you make a fancy E,

Who's that girl?
Who has bruises all over her legs because she is in fact the clumsiest person on this planet,

Who's that girl?
Who wants to live in Fiji when she grows up and has actually tried a ham, jam, cocoa powder, Doritos and spreadable cheese sandwich,

Who's that girl?
That likes to dance crazy and once cracked her head open by a yellow tractor,

Who's that girl?
That tried snails before and thought they were delicious and has been touched on the shoulder by Prince Andrew, so technically she is royal,

Well, that person is me,
I am who I am,
You can never change who you are,
Because you are you, it sounds confusing but it's true,
So who's that girl . . .
Well that's me, myself and I.

Emily Mundon (13)
Barlby High School, Barlby

Football

F antastic fans chanting songs.
O n the field, the action is beginning.
O utside of the stadium, the burger vans are getting ready for the hungry half-time hooligans.
T rumpeting horns billowing around the stadium.
B alls flying in and out of the pitch from the exhausted players.
A whistle blows and it's all over.
L ots of shouts and lots of arguments.
L et's go home.

Dan Bushby (14)
Barlby High School, Barlby

Uncle Michael

His smiling blue eyes,
His huge jug ears.
Who could tell that it would end in tears?

His sly little jokes,
His comforting words.
Who knew that it would hurt?

Always a smile on his
Small, slight face.
Who could tell that he was losing a race?

Always a drink in his
Shaking left hand.
Why was he shaking? We didn't understand.

Those stories he told
About the travels he made.
Who knew that his life was
Starting to fade?

It all ended the day of
Friday the 13th.

We held a wake and a glass was raised,
'To dear Uncle Mike and the good old days'.

Those smiling blue eyes,
Those huge jug ears,
Those sly little jokes,
Those comforting words,
Those stories he told
About the travels he made.

I'm so sorry, Uncle Mike, that we
Could do nothing but sit back and watch,
As you let your own life fade.

Amescia Queenan (14)
Barlby High School, Barlby

The Howl Of The Wind

The spray of water
Soaking to the skin
Temporarily blinding you
Wipe away the water and the onslaught re-begins

The speed and the power
Driving you on
Building and building
Forever going on

The howl of the wind
As it rushed past your face
Buffering your features
And keeping up the pace

The ferocity of the waves
Lifting you up as you ride upon
Before dropping you from nowhere
Then you climb the next one

The cold of the water
As the boat is tipped
And you splash into the drink
The sailing equivalent of falling when you trip

Pulling the boat up
And climbing back in
The truth dawns on you
That you must do all that work again.

But when you think to yourself
Of what is to happen
You realise that that work and that hassle
Is exactly what you want.

Jack Hanslope (14)
Barlby High School, Barlby

The Flow Of Football

The freshly cut grass,
The gentle breeze blows,
The rush of anticipation,
Gushes and flows.

Lining up on the field,
One by one,
Banter from the crowd,
A game no one would bet on.

The howl of the whistle,
Lets all hell break loose,
As an early foul is just ignored,
The fans shout abuse.

A howler from the keeper,
Puts them right in the game,
The home fans rejoice,
As he hangs his head in shame.

As the end grew near,
One last attack,
The ball came in,
As the defenders stood back.

The ball on his head,
The goal a sure-fire thing,
As it struck the netting,
With a thunderous ping.

The game ends,
With a one-one draw,
An exciting thriller,
Or a boring yawn?

Leo Wright (13)
Barlby High School, Barlby

Bonfire Night

As I walk up to the field
There's a bright orange light
It flickers at the top
But motionless at the bottom
As I walk over the twigs and mud
The light starts to get larger
I feel a wind of heat hit my face
Suddenly there are noises
Bangs and pops with ear-piercing screeches
At first it's frightening
But the excitement takes over
The nearer I get
The more people I see
Children writing with sparklers
Toffee apples all around
The smell of soup and jacket potatoes too
Then it's time for the rockets
Whoosh! Up the crowd cheer with amazement
Something catches my eye
A life-like figure sat on a chair
Melting in the chair with sparks flying off
Warmth killing the cold colourful sky
As the night comes to an end
The once bright light turns to a dim glow
Leaving the crowd with just a memory
Of gunpowder, treason and plot and the figure
Who brought the 5th November
Which is always going to be one date to
Remember.

Brooke Patrick (13)
Barlby High School, Barlby

And That's What Family Is About

Your mum, your dad
The ones that brought you up
The ones you love the most of all
The two most special people in the world
The ones you would do anything for
That's what family is about.

Your brothers and sisters
The ones that annoy you the most
The ones you love to annoy
The ones you love to hate
The ones that stick up for you in tough times
That's what family is about.

Your grandmas and grandads
The ones that look after you when your parents start partying
The ones that take you in when tragedies happen
The ones that have the TV on maximum volume
The ones you laugh at when they start to nod
That's what family is about.

The ones you have lost
The ones that were snatched away
The ones you will forever miss
The ones you will forever remember
The ones you will forever love
That's what family is about.

Matthew Williamson (14)
Barlby High School, Barlby

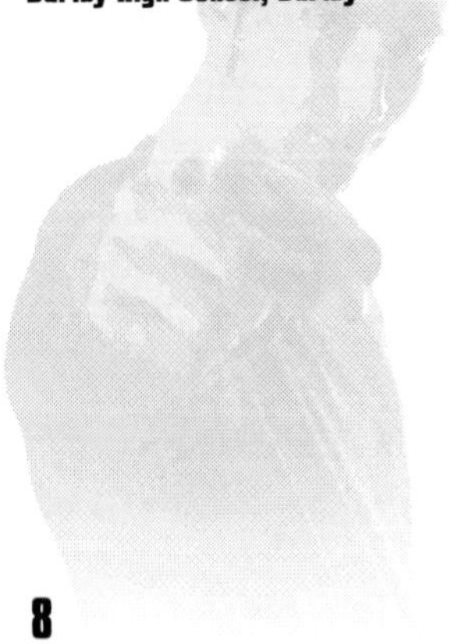

Day . . . After . . . Day

Day after day, the work never stops,
Through English, maths and science your pen never drops,
The coursework carries on page after page,
Then another essay on the feeling of rage,
The book fills and the ink dries out,
But it's still not enough to avoid the shout,
Day after day.

The bell rings and school is done,
Huge relief as you put down the gun,
You head on home, hoping to relax,
But you arrive and down comes the axe,
A huge pile of questions and worksheets,
All that homework that's built up over the weeks,
You fall to the ground and pray to God,
Please vanish, I won't find it odd,
Day after day.

Every day the work doesn't finish,
Why can't it go away with just one wish,
Life was created for people to work,
Why can't I be free like a fish or a hawk?
Day after day the work never stops,
Day after day.

Frazer Levett (14)
Barlby High School, Barlby

Racism Poem

R epeated words in my face, that is all around me.
A sense of hatred fills inside me.
C an't ignore it. It is all around me.
I try to run away from it, but it haunts me.
S eems to be everywhere I go. It just keeps hurting me.
M y mind says to me . . . 'Why is it all aimed at me?'

Liam Hubel (14)
Barlby High School, Barlby

Untitled

How will I ever feel love and affection,
    After all this?
The shouts and the cries, the evil looks and the lies,
    My parents never loved each other, how could I?
Always ignored, and never important,
    I sometimes wish they just had me aborted.
I would hide in my bedroom to block out the noise, my brother's ears in my hands,
    Those poor little boys.
'We're doing it for you,' is what they would say,
    'What have I done wrong, why do I have to pay?'
They fought over money, over me and my brothers,
    Was it just us, or could there be others?
I knew we weren't normal, weren't families supposed to love?
    I even often thought, I'd be better up above.
Maybe I would learn to love, maybe that's just what I need,
    To get away from this house, away from all the greed.
I knew I was trapped, and became suicidal,
    What happened to the good life, where a parent is an idol?
I wanted to leave, and never go back.
    How will I ever feel love and affection,
        After all this?

Courteney Parker (14)
Barlby High School, Barlby

Sisters

S trings grasp them strong;
I t bonds two friends.
S hell of outer disguises;
T he passion from within.
E ach strive for a soaring rank.
R ealising an eternal companion;
S trings grasp them strong.

Heather Allison (14)
Barlby High School, Barlby

Attitude

There was a kid at my school
People thought he was a fool
His name was Gav
He acted like a chav
He wore a big hoodie
And it was all muddy
He lived on a large estate
With his mother and her mate
The word was they took drugs
But that game is just for mugs
People thought he was a thug
And he had a dog called Doug
He walked with a swagger
With a face like a dagger
People gave him a wide birth
And I thought what on earth?
He is only a boy with an attitude
And comes over cocky and rude
If he was sent in the right direction
And given some affection
That could be all that it takes
And he could make some good mates!

Alex Barraclough (14)
Barlby High School, Barlby

Teenage Soldier

S tranded
O rdnance
L ives lost
D eath
I mmoral
E xpendable
R eload.

Harry Wallis (13)
Barlby High School, Barlby

Life!

Seeing things through different eyes
Can never capture all the lies
All the deceiving, all the pain.
Acting like you could be just a bit sane.

Paths and decisions that you think of in your head.
Can always change like cold broken lead
When someone close to you dies
Is there any rule to follow, do you abide?

And the love you share with someone close
Does that change things, do they care the most?
The tears you cry when bad things occur
Always makes things fuzzy, they're always a blur.

But when they leave, what do you have?
If not someone who starts to laugh
I know the feeling so deep, deep down
That turns a smile to a frown.

The hollow feeling in your heart
Is taken away and ripped apart
Change a view deep in your mind
And it only takes you just a little time to find.

Tara Marshall (14)
Barlby High School, Barlby

Illness

I sit there watching, watching her pain,
All those drugs flowing to her veins,
I sit there staring, staring at her smile,
I don't know how she's lasted all this while,
I sit there hearing her cry, hearing her voice saying, 'Why oh why?'
I try to be a good sister, I really do but I can't change nature,
Otherwise I would have it instead of *you!*

Tyla Hughes (13)
Barlby High School, Barlby

Memories Of A Mother

I still remember your laughter,
The proud warm beam that shone across your face.
You watched me grow and learn,
Guiding me through life at a steady pace.

You were there at the beginning,
Letting my tiny little hand wrap round one fat finger.
You're there now kissing me goodbye as I prepare to leave,
But on the doorstep I just stop. Just linger.

I remember the days when we kicked the ball at the park,
I'd run with loose laces as I found tying them tricky.
I remember being in your arms as you wiped away my tears,
You told me not to worry about that stupid boy Nicky.

You stood by me and held my hand,
Whilst I opened the results of my final exams.
You tucked the lost curl behind my ear on my big day,
Soon showing off my baby scans.

I know that you've been there for me,
And you're still gonna be there every single day.
But now I must learn and see what it's like,
And look after my little Daisy May.

Bryony Ledger (15)
Barlby High School, Barlby

My Day

S lavery
C haotic
H ell
O bsolence
O bey
L ifeless.

Kieran Gray (14)
Barlby High School, Barlby

Why Do They Treat Me So Different?

Everybody sees me, I stand out from the crowd,
When everyone's around, I cannot be proud.
I feel so very different; I'll never be the same,
I've different coloured skin and an unusual name.
Why do they treat me so different?

All them names you say, I hear,
You and all your friends, I fear.
Inside I'm just the same as you,
But you treat me like something on your shoe.
Why do they treat me so different?

While all the other children play,
I sit alone every day.
They never let me join in,
And stay away like I've been in the bin.
Why do they treat me so different?

At night I sit and cry,
Wishing that I could go and die.
They post rude letters through the door,
And roughly push me to the floor.
Why do they treat me so different?

Georgia Brooks (13)
Barlby High School, Barlby

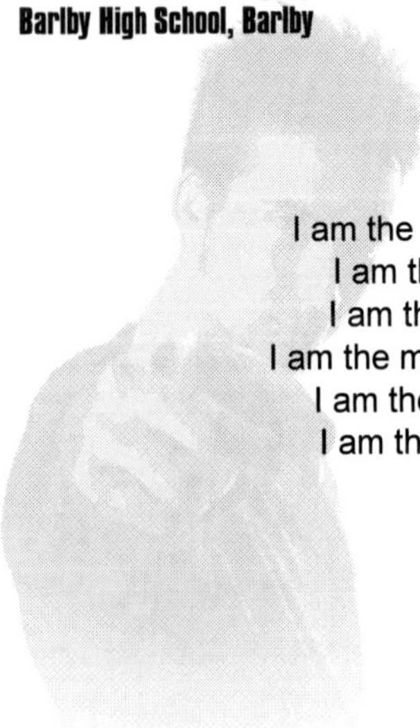

I Am The Horse

I am the hooves that plough the ground,
I am the tail that makes the sound,
I am the eyes that stalk the danger,
I am the mouth that eats out of the manger,
I am the face that intrigues the buyer,
I am the legs that jump much higher,
I am the horse,
And I am the rider.

Eve Headley (13)
Barlby High School, Barlby

The Best Thing In Life

Having fun and having friends,
And hoping the night never ends.
Is the best thing in life.

Going out and being young,
With the taste of booze against my tongue.
Is the best thing in life.

Going to parties when they are wild,
And when the atmosphere is far from mild.
Is the best thing in life.

Getting drunk, my heart then sunk,
As I thought of that tragic night,
When my friend had that awful fight.

There was blood on the floor as we left through the door of the hospital.
He had been stabbed and his wounds were dabbed.

They checked his heartbeat, it was there no more.
But I know my friend is through Heaven's door.

It was all down to drink I know and think,
That now it is not the best thing in life.

Liam Ware-Wilkinson (14)
Barlby High School, Barlby

Hoodie

H ooligan
O ffensive
O ffensive
D eadly
I mmature
E xciting.

Josh Stapp (14)
Barlby High School, Barlby

Stranger Danger

Today I saw a man
He drove by in his white van

He stopped at the lights
I walked by, he gave me the frights

Offered me a lift
Seemingly a pleasant gift

I opened the door
Within seconds I'm on the floor

I'm bundled in the bay
To no affray

Fear and terror cloud my mind
How can the world be this unkind?

Then the destination was unclear
Now I know I was to lose all I hold dear

For now I write to you from up high
Never let a stranger feed you a lie.

Jonathan Adamson (14)
Barlby High School, Barlby

This Is My World

Sick of feeling pushed around,
Would feel better if I had friends around.

Sometimes happy, sometimes sad,
Sometimes throw tantrums, feel bad.

Mum and Dad don't seem to care less.
Grandma's in her own happiness.

They're not in my world
So what do they know?
Teenage years, I wish they'd go!

Paige Tudor (14)
Barlby High School, Barlby

Nothing But A Lover

Meeting your eyes, I sense such a beautiful mystery,
Being the power of your sight where I read a history,
About the love and life that shines through your eyes,
About the empire you praise through passionate nights.

There at the depth of your scene, too much to suffice,
Bold skies under melting mountains made of ice,
Where silver covers the soft soil and hard dice.

Reading between unreadable pages of your book,
Leaping beats lack the power to even steal
Or to run down the rivers rippling the mouths of lust,
Where my dreams dive and then rust through dust,
Then exceedingly fly about your blue airy gust.

And at the depth of your looks, and the meadows of your voice,
Millions of beats bow for the tenderness with extreme rejoice,
Yet the perils of your heart, looks too bright to fake,
And with my heart being homeless, it's a bit too unworthy,
To take . . . beneath mine which is too weak, not to break.

Kayleigh Williams (13)
Barlby High School, Barlby

Clouds

Like white candyfloss in the sky.
Turning slowly as we pass by.
Obstacles for aeroplanes
Dodging in and out
Things that look like
Faces and objects we watch
As we walk about.
Sneakily hiding the sunshine
But that's all the weather we would like,
Clouds, clouds, clouds we see
All day and night,

Olivia Gabb (11)
Barlby High School, Barlby

Life

You can't choose it.
Who you are,
Your family,
Your friends,
You could be poor,
Or you could be rich.
Your looks,
Your personality,
Who you hate,
Or who you fall in love with,
Everyone cries,
But everyone will smile at one point,
Because when you are sad,
And need a shoulder to cry on,
You should always know,
That everything will be alright in the end.
And if it's not alright,
It is not yet the end!

Sarah Bramley (13)
Barlby High School, Barlby

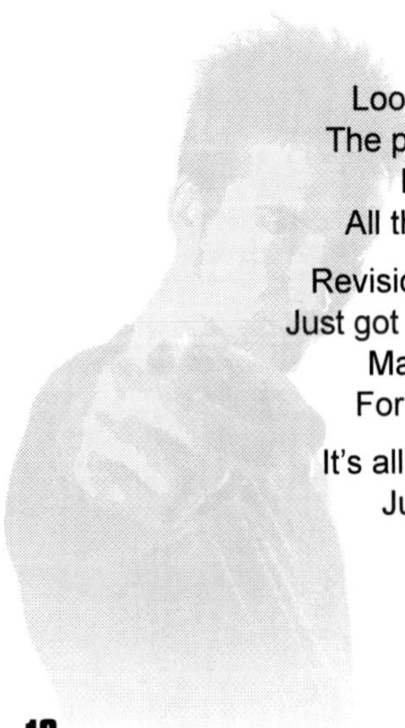

Study

Look in all the books you have
The pressure on it makes you sad
Early to rise, late to bed
All this work, it hurts your head.

Revision, revision, that's all they say
Just got to make it till the end of the day
Making sure that I'm not late
For the results I've got to wait.

It's all about the grades these days
Just so we will all get paid.

Katie Neal (13)
Barlby High School, Barlby

Ups And Downs

Life has its ups and downs.
You lose people that are very close to you.
That's happened to me twice.
One minute they're there,
The next they're gone forever.

It was just a normal night,
I thought everything was OK.
Then I get woken up
And get told the news.
I don't believe it.
One minute he was there, now he's not.
I'll never see him again,
But I know he will be watching every move I make.
The memories will last forever.
And I will never forget him,
There's always that hurt and upset inside,
But life goes on . . .

Erin Clark (14)
Barlby High School, Barlby

Turtle

Turtle, turtle in the sea
What have you ever done for me

Swimming round in the dark sea
Is he trying to replace me?

Swimming round an enormous creature
It's a shame I couldn't see its features

The turtle swims towards the shore
He's not giving up, trying more and more

In the distance I can see
The turtle must really need me.

Daniel Jackson (14)
Barlby High School, Barlby

From A Troubled Mind

Lo and behold, my friends are smoking again
I hide in my cave, my bedroom, my den.
Jesus walks through the forest where I buried my friends
Where will I go to make my amends?

I can't sleep tonight
The shadows on my bedroom wall write.
Time will pass and I will grow
Into something I don't know.

Laughter chills the night air
And the colour of despair is in my hair.
My name is miserable and full of regret
And I'm praying to God I've never met.

I walk to school with my shoes tied tight
I walk to school after that restless night.
I'm not sure who I will be
If I die lonely, at least I'll be free.

Harry Pulleyne (14)
Barlby High School, Barlby

My Cat Maud

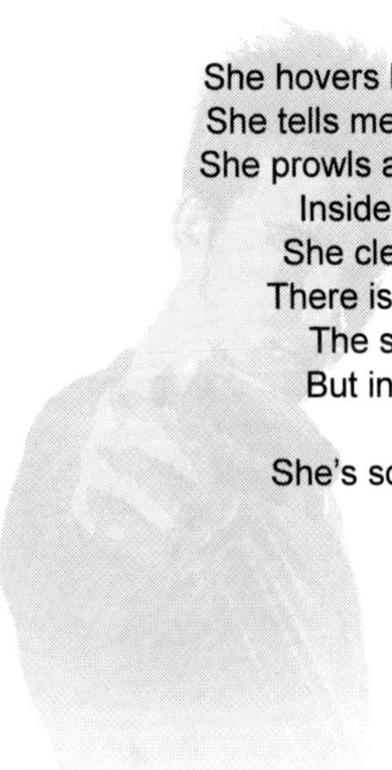

She hovers by the cupboard where her food is kept.
She tells me, in her own language, what she wants.
She prowls about the garden, but not far from home.
Inside she grooms her paws and claws.
She cleans her fur till it glistens like glass.
There is a warm spot left where she's been.
The sunshine is where she likes to be.
But inside, looking out, safe and warm.
She's gentle but fierce.
She's soft but timid and frightened at times.
My job is to care for her.
My cat Maud.

Calum Finn (14)
Barlby High School, Barlby

The Referee

He gets yelled abuse and told he's blind,
Though this man he doesn't mind.
He gets insulted and called names,
This isn't appreciated during his games.

A nasty tackle goes in from behind,
But the linesman said the penalty was denied.
Instead the boss shows a red but before that a yellow,
Off you go you dirty fellow.

The insults fly in from everywhere,
'Look, I got the ball you blind mare.'
Players sprint to him in huge clans,
Before he knows it he is encircled by players and fans.

The abuse roars and the chants wail,
They're basically calling him a fail.
But it's not his fault, it's part of the job,
Except standing up to the angry yob.

Katie Parker (15)
Barlby High School, Barlby

Winter

Snuggling on the settee watching TV
Oh how I love the way you hold me
Your strong arms keep me warm
If I'm with you I don't care if there's a storm
As the fire crackles and roars
The rain outside rapidly pours
As I lie here thinking about our future together
I know you will always be my good weather
I will forget this never
You will be in my heart forever.

Holly Dack (13)
Barlby High School, Barlby

Skate Poem

Skateboard, music, long black hair.
'Emo,' you shout. Why label me?

Earphones in. Bullet for my valentine I think.
'Mosher,' you shout. Why label me?

I get to the skatepark.
'Woodpusher,' you shout. Why label me?

My friends turn up, we head to the shop.
An old person walks past.
'You lot best split up, we don't want any break-ins.'
Why label me?

'Yes you are, you're wearing hoodies,'
She said. Why label me?

'No, we wear hoodies because it's cold. Not because we're going to stab you!'
Why label us?

Brandon Glover (13)
Barlby High School, Barlby

My Poem

I walked in the front door thinking everything was OK
When all of a sudden I saw a bouquet,
The card on the side said it all,
Then the phone rang with an awful call,
Mum cried, 'The dog is gone,'
I ran to my room and wrote a song,
I read it out to Mum and Dad,
They both broke down and were really sad,
No one knows how I am feeling and no one understands.

Eve Chapman (13)
Barlby High School, Barlby

A Bloody Brilliant Idea

The flesh
Of my dreams strewn across the desk
. . . now where has that answer fled?
Pinch the
Words and chain them together
Now under that solitary pencil nib, there's an idea
Writhing

And where that nimble idea spills
Her heart,
The paper
Stains
Red and gold
The punishment of defying
The author is fulfilled
Until the next
Full stop.

Stephanie Heaven-Terry (14)
Barlby High School, Barlby

Friends

A friend is someone,
Who will always be there,
Someone who will give you,
Comfort and care.

Share the laughs,
Share the tears,
All the moods,
All the fears.

To sum this up,
It needs to be said,
If I had no friends,
My soul would be dead!

Lucy Wylie (14)
Barlby High School, Barlby

Does He Love Me?

He is supposed to love me,
But I'm not quite sure,
He loves him more,
But love is pure,
He only loves a certain type,
But that is not mine,
He says those words that make me cry,
But he seems to think I'm fine,
Life is hard for me,
Knowing how he feels,
And me knowing,
That this is real,
What's wrong with me?
What did I do wrong?
Why doesn't he love me?
I'll never know . . .

Danielle Preston (13)
Barlby High School, Barlby

The Test

I am a super intelligent alien mind.
One look at my brain and I'm sure you will find
A wondrous box of mathematical wonder.
Full of sun, not rain and thunder.
I finish my test with ages to spare.
In fact I start styling my hair.
I swagger to the front, smug look on my face.
The other kids know that I won the test race.
Teacher starts marking, we can see his pen smoking.
We all laugh when Billy starts choking.
The teacher puts his pen down.
Looks at me with a frown
And says I got 20%!

Daniel Price (14)
Barlby High School, Barlby

School Sucks

From nine till half past three,
Work all day with no sleep.

Get up in the morning,
Just get up and go.
Come to the gate,
And let everyone know.

I'm here,
Just another day,
I really can't stand it,
Let me just say:

I don't think you know,
Who I really am.
So stop judging me,
In the way you think you can.

Eleanor Steele (14)
Barlby High School, Barlby

Come On England

Come on England! Come on England!
Get it right this time,
Always knew it, you can do it,
Get it in your mind.

Come on Gerrard! Come on Rooney!
Everybody's here,
Come on Terry! Come on Lampard!
Nothing left to fear.

You can make it! You can take it!
Never mind the rest,
Come on Theo! Come on Rio!
Come and do your best.

Samuel Horsley (13)
Barlby High School, Barlby

The Circus

Clowns fire animals,
Definitely not camels,

Fire burning in the air,
Magic tricks everywhere,

Clowns making funny faces,
And even tripping over their own laces.

Mostly young, mostly old,
Well that's what we've been told,

Audience up, audience down,
Making sure they're not too loud,

Burning hoops,
Blazing fire,
Let's hear it for Coco, the one and only clown we hired!

Victoria Moughan (12)
Barlby High School, Barlby

Come Back

It's been six months, eight days, twelve hours too long
Barely making it through these midnights popping love songs.
Trying to figure out, right, where we went so wrong
So long, I ain't ready for goodbye yet,
Nights so cold only you could change the climate.
Come back, Jay Z didn't make hits
Your side or mine, we're designed to be adjacent,
Face it, I was your favourite, vice versa,
Go search for a new boy who might jerk you, might,
Hurt you and leave you in the dirt.
I'll keep you on my heart like a white T-shirt,
I won't hurt you again, you'll be safe from that,
I'll be there protecting you like a baseball bat.

Isaac Wass (14)
Barlby High School, Barlby

Not Knowing Me

The days go by
With a flick of a fly
And people don't know about me
And don't understand what I could be,
It's not every day you meet people like me
Thinking all the time,
Wondering what to do
Don't worry
I'm doing it for you!

Emma Tune (14)
Barlby High School, Barlby

Racism

R uthless blasphemy
A nger
C ulture abuse
I nvalid views
S lave trade and cruelty
M ade outcasts.

Jordan Cox (14)
Barlby High School, Barlby

Exams

E ducation
X tra lessons
A fraid of failing
M aths revision
S ilent working.

Eric Garside (14)
Barlby High School, Barlby

The Scrum

R ucking over getting hurt
U pset and devastation when you lose
G lad and delighted when we win
B ut we will always try
Y et another dodgy ref, yet another dodgy decision.

Scott Hunt (13)
Barlby High School, Barlby

Freefall

Freefall.
Down, down, down.
Into the unknown.
No one pushed me.
There's no one there to catch me.
Floating.
Falling, floating, flying.
The place between Heaven and Hell.
One moment.
An instant that can determine life or death.
What's there to live for?
What's the point in dying?
Limbo.
Stranded.
Waiting.
3, 2, 1.
What happens now?

Megan Pinches (18)
Bede Sixth Form, Billingham

Suicide Love

I don't believe you're here
Nor do I believe you're there
I believe you're in-between
Just watching over with care

You never failed to lighten my day
But now you're gone.
We were once classed as two
Now there's only one.

Nothing feels the same
And I miss you more than I can say
I feel helpless and alone
I wish there was a way.

I pretend nothing is wrong
I'm living in a dream
I need you here with me
Nothing is how it should be it would seem.

It appears I have one way out
But is this right?
I can't be sure
But being with you is the perfect sight.

So here I go my love
I will soon be yours
No pain is felt, only relief
As I'm walking through the doors.

Holly Burton (17)
Bede Sixth Form, Billingham

A Sonnet To My Shadow

Wherever you go you will find me;
My seemingly eternal friend in life.
A friend so hard to bear;
A tryst so filled with strife.
I've seen the future, and it seems so bright;
But still she lingers in the dark;
Unwilling to die without a fight.
You won't see hide nor hair of her, she leaves no mark;
But still she haunts my dreams.
They label her 'anxiety'.
They treat me; try to rip her apart at the seams;
I won't let her define me.

One day she will be dead; I only hope before I am done.
This battle will be won.

Sian Chloe Crookston (16)
Bede Sixth Form, Billingham

Mermaids

Battling fishnets, she slowly sank down.
Another fish dead.
But overnight a transformation . . .
She grew up tall and her scales turned into a long
Neon tail, glowing amongst the shadows.
Her gills grew into long blonde hair, flowing freely
In the silent sea.
Her large grey eyes now beautiful and blue,
Searching out preying eyes.
She floated down through a hole in the rock, and
Inside a place of unbelievable enchantment.
The mermaids had taken her to their kingdom.

Lottie Monks (10)
Giggleswick School, Giggleswick

Balance

As you tripped,
I picked you up.

As you ate,
I provided.

As you became upset,
I was sanctuary.

As I became lost,
You found me.

As I fell ill,
You were hope.

As I passed away,
You mourned.

This is balance.
Balance.

Ben Phillips (13)
Ian Ramsey CE School, Stockton-on-Tees

I'm The Person

I'm the person you smirked at,
I'm the person who worked hard,
I'm the person you laughed at,
I'm the person you called names,
I'm the person nobody liked.
Why?
No reason, no difference between us!
Look at me now.
Then look at you.
Now there's a difference!

Abbie Stoddart (14)
Ian Ramsey CE School, Stockton-on-Tees

The Shelter

Huddling in the shelter,
Like penguins in an igloo.
Wind howling mournfully,
Its presence felt hauntingly.

Freezing in the shelter,
Spewing mist from my lips.
Ice in the air,
Mingling with my hair.

Waiting in the shelter,
Staring at my watch,
Time dragging on,
We've been here too long.

Hope in the shelter,
The bus is here!

Dylan Whitaker (13)
Ian Ramsey CE School, Stockton-on-Tees

The Exam

The exam is gruelling, brutal and tough,
Feeds on the disappointment of those not good enough.

The exam leaves people with beautiful bright smiles,
Or deprives those of a future worthwhile.

The exam is a journey, which portrays life,
Your journey may end, like this poem,
This line.

Charlie Oxenham (13)
Ian Ramsey CE School, Stockton-on-Tees

Torn

You love me, I deserve to be hated,
I cherish you, and for your love I waited,
Your kind ways and warm heart I adore,
I give you what I have,
You won't ask for more.

Your gentle advice allows me to flourish,
For all of my sins, let me be punished.
When I feel cold, you make me feel warm,
I cannot balance, you leave me torn,
My fear is that I give you my trust,
Give me yours in return,
You really must.

Just one remark and I am gone,
Not a word, yet I just want one,
Please, just alter your ways for me,
Please, just say the word,
I'll make you see,
I love you simply for who you are,
Not who you want to be,
Try as I may, I will never succeed,
Loving you like I do is my only sin of greed.

Amber Southall (12)
Macmillan Academy, Middlesbrough

You And I

I love you but I love you not.
You make me feel so insecure.
I feel the cold when it is hot.
Although I'm rich, you make me poor.
My ears and eyes block out the star.
The rage I feel turns into fear.
I love you just the way you are.
You make me laugh, I shed a tear.
I let you in, you let me out.
You make me wait what seems an age.
You fill me up with lots of doubt.
You trap me in my lonely cage.
I love you but I love you not.
You break my heart a lot, a lot.

Joely Clark (12)
Macmillan Academy, Middlesbrough

Autumn Is Here

Like a thousand dancing dragons,
Red, yellow and brown,
Swirling through the air in fiery splendour,
Carried like feathers upon the icy breeze.
A spiralling flame descending from the canopies of trees,
To land on the ground,
A crunchy carpet along the streets.
Grey skies and bitter winds,
Raindrops falling like diamonds,
Glittering as they fall.
Chestnuts, green and spiky like hedgehogs,
Or brown and shiny, ready to be gathered by children.
Fog descending upon houses and cars,
Clinging to the streets, a fine misty blanket,
Autumn is here.

Billy Rowbotham (12)
Manor CE School, York

Love Bird

Fly away little bird, fly
Spread your wings and fly
Spread the love from your song
Make it heard across the globe
Thread the notes carefully, make them smile
And if you need to little bird, give them a little cry.

Once you have left the nest
You'll be on your own
But you will find him
Your one and only
You will treat him well and he will treat you well
You won't be scum, neither will he
He'll support you
Lift you
And fly alongside you.

You will make the nest yourself
Just like the one I made you
You will be thankful
You will be gracious
And you will be, well, me.

Then those protective shells will break
You will be tired but glad
And he'll support you
Lift you
And fly alongside you

Then you will feel the pain I felt
When they ask you to leave
But you will have to agree so they can sing their song

So please little bird
Sing carefully, sing proud
And loud
But remember the love I carried for you
And pass the love to the ones you love most
My love bird.

Ellie Norris (12)
Manor CE School, York

The York Train

This the York train, leaving the station,
Heading towards its destination,
Clickety-clack, clickety-clack,
This is the York train on the track,

The morning sun, rising up in the sky,
Watching the fluffy clouds gently fly,
Clickety-clack, clickety-clack,
This is the York train on the track,

Buildings and churches racing past,
We're on the move, we're going fast,
Clickety-clack, clickety-clack,
This is the York train on the track,

Into the country, now steaming along,
Listen to the train singing its song,
Clickety-clack, clickety-clack,
This is the York train on the track,

A majestic deer eating the grass,
By the sparkling river as we pass,
Clickety-clack, clickety-clack,
This is the York train on the track,

See the field of barley and rye,
Swaying in the wind as we rush by,
Clickety-clack, clickety-clack,
This is the York train on the track,

Waving people in the park,
Stars glitter, it's getting dark,
Clickety-clack, clickety-clack,
This is the York train on the track,

The moon shines down on the line below,
In the spotlight, you're the star of the show,
Clickety-clack, clickety-clack,
This is the York train on the track,

Getting closer, nearer now, slowing down,
Steaming tiredly, into the seaside town,
Clickety-clack, clickety-clack,
This is the York train on the track,

Nine o'clock, we're bang on time,
No delays along the line,
Clickety-clack, clickety-clack,
This is the York train on the track,

This is the York train entering the station,
This is the York train, at its destination,
Clickety-clack, clickety-clack,
That was the York train on the track!

Sophie Nicholls (12)
Manor CE School, York

On A Cold Dark Night

On a cold, dark night,
Down a cold, dark alley,
In a cold, dark world,
I got taken away.
Away from my family,
Away from my home,
Where were they taking me?
Why didn't anyone help me?
They said I'd never go back.
This was my new home.
I wanted to leave, to go back home.
I tried to run, tried to hide,
They caught me, brought me back,
Whipped me,
On a cold, dark night someone found me,
Brought me back,
Back to my family,
Back to my home.

Mary Paterson (12)
Manor CE School, York

Africa

They are deprived of our riches
Yet we miss out on their spirit raising group
I wish I could wipe away our world's stitches
Someone please tie the loop

Starving silently in a corner of a squashed room
Selflessly trying to put on a brave face for their ill mother
Suffering inside like a forgotten tomb
Holding hands with another brother

At night the mother cries for her children and their dying father
Looking at the creaking floorboards where her eight children lie
Where would you rather choose to live?
It's got to change, as a family we can't let our brothers and sisters die

To think no one will ever feel the burden they share
As I reach to shake a small girl's hand she hesitates for a second
Wiping her palms ferociously like she'd heard I care
Watching her burning shame being beckoned
It hurt me deeply like blood behind a bruise
Is it right to just let them lose?

And her brother is watching me forlornly
He limps forward, self consciously protecting her
She watches him adoringly
Like he's the wise man offering myrrh

His story is a tragedy, a tale too long for this
In our world he could have been treated in a flash
But now he'll never walk right and all those adventures he'll miss
That thought may always bother him like a permanent rash

This all made my soul cry
I'm not going to lie
They cannot die
This is the last sigh

Just to make them smile would be an incredible gift
Spirit rising roots would plant a fruitful tree in my soul
That glimpse of a song would be such a lift
Then another human would be playing that role

I would love . . . to give a thousand hugs to any one of them in pain
I would love . . . to buy a million presents for every single child
And keep every single mother sane

But I know I can't, even if I was rich . . . not on my own!
More love in our hearts will celebrate us
Like giving a child an ice cream with a special chocolate cone.

Bitterness replaced with sweetness would be good because . . .
We are all superstars so let's pretend for a moment I am the moon.
I am the moon: I surround myself with stars.

Anna Wade (11)
Manor CE School, York

World War I Poem

(Inspired by 'Dulce Et Decorum Est' by Wilfred Owen)

The cold wind blew, slicing like a knife,
Bullets blazed overhead, men started running, like a child from a nightmare.
The bullets fought against the wind, the wounded clinging onto life.
And men fell, we started to despair.
Scared soldiers ducked into a trench,
Shallow, ragged came out their breaths,
The crumbling earth their hands would clench,
Hoping not to be among the many deaths.

Move! Move! - The cry echoed through the field,
Men dived, fought like crazed animals, running from danger,
They forgot the weapons, like guns on the floor, ones we once did wield,
The bomb landed softly, exploding,
But the silence that followed was even stranger.
Captains spoke with such high zest,
To soldiers hoping for some glory,
The words I wish I'd never said: Dulce et decorum est,
Pro patria mori.

Danielle Greaves (13)
Manor CE School, York

The Chase

Everyone could see,
The fugitives flee,

They took off like a bee from a flower,
In their legs, they must have had power.

The police couldn't catch them,
The FBI couldn't catch them.

None of them could,
No one else would.

But I can,
And I did.

I went like a track star,
Flew past every house and car.

I ran with grace and perfection,
Without any detection.

I saw them stop at a house,
I ran as quiet as a mouse.

They went inside,
I decided to hide.

They came out and looked around,
I jumped on them, my heart began to pound.

I caught them,
I knew I could.

Victoria Watson (13)
Manor CE School, York

What Matters To Me

The world should stay a beautiful place
With butterflies flying
No babies crying
Peaceful

Peace must erode into every way of life
Making the world war free
No bombs dropping
Peaceful

Walk in the dew in the early morn
Glistening are the spiderwebs
Not a soul around
Peaceful

By light seeping through the window
Wake up from deep sleep
Smile, not everyone can
Peaceful

These things are the little things in life
But they matter to me
Because not everyone has them
So they matter to me.

Eilidh Rivers (11)
Manor CE School, York

The Lady Of Shalott

(Inspired by 'The Lady of Shalott' by Alfred Lord Tennyson)

He looked upon the town laid bare
From atop his jet black mare
His heart was filled with great despair
For the people that had died there
He vowed to bring down Arthur
Answering to his burning passion
He set to work, a bow did fashion
From the wood burnt and ashen
A single arrow meant for Arthur

Riding swift and fast and light
He came upon Camelot by Morning Bright
He rode through gates tall with might
And headed for Arthur, his prize in sight
He vowed to bring down Arthur
Darkness fell across the land
The hooded man had bow in hand
No man dared stir in that land
Checkmate it looked for Arthur

Moving slowly through the crowd
The man walked, using them to shroud
His hidden target, he would not be cowed
Arthur stands tall, strong and proud
An easy target was Arthur
He drew his bow, he aimed and fired
He stepped back into Muddy Mire
He ran thro' the pub, past knight and squire
Moving like the floor was fire
Heard a shout from near the spire
'There's the knave that shot the sire'
Now the hunt was hot and dire
In the favour of the sire

He saw the gates, seeming higher
Than the time he'd seen them prior
Then before him was the sire
'Missed,' said the man
Called Arthur.

David Gwynne (13)
Manor CE School, York

What Matters To Me?

W riting
H umours
A cting
T aunting people

M ilkshakes
A ppearance
T yping
T echnology
E lderly
R ugby
S ummer

T apes
O ctober

M y iPod Touch
E ating.

Henry Simpson-Lucas (11)
Manor CE School, York

Differences

Eating out of
Gold plates,
Eating out of
Wooden plates
The fresh fish caught this morning,
The four-day-old squelchy bread
To feed a family
Of six
A day of relaxation over
The steaming yellow ball,
Working all day
In the infested mud
As rain pats on their backs,

The warm comfy bed
Sleeping in sound
Nothing to disturb,
Lying on the dead murky grey
Floor
Baby's cry
Everywhere
Cramped up next to the
Wall,

Warm water slides through your
Hair,
Squat down in the filth surrounded
By greenery
Looking into the opaque dead
Smelling water
Splash as it covers their face
A weekly wash for them,

Clean and healthy free of
Disease
Money seeping out of their
Pockets,
Money is a rare word for them
As disease fills up inside their
Very soul
Slowly it plunges into their heart
Slowly the breathing stops
Slowly their life is taken.

George Dodd (13)
Manor CE School, York

My Winning Poem

I am here today to tell you all about
What really matters to me

Animals
I love them

They matter to me because
Technically we are animals too

We are mammals
And I care about humans
And animals

Teachers are humans
And I care about humans

Everyone,
Everything
I care about everything.

Emily Groom-White (12)
Manor CE School, York

Broken

Do you know what it feels like
To be
Broken?

Broken on the inside
Broken on the outside
It shows in your eyes
The hurt, the sadness, the distress

Broken like a mirror
The shards lying everywhere
Glittering pieces of glass
Unwanted, disliked, alone

Broken in the body
Torn at the soul
Ripped at the heart
And the pain, it hurts so

It won't fix
The pain is stubborn
It won't leave
Too much, too much to fight

I've tried Blu-Tack
I've tried Sellotape
Even tried glue . . .
But nothing will fix it

Broken
In so many pieces
Too many choices, too many decisions
What, oh what, am I to do?

Do you know what it feels like
To be
Broken?

All that matters most
Is that
I am fixed.

Samantha Eastwood (12)
Manor CE School, York

What Matters To Me?

S illy little chicks hatch,
P retty pink flowers bloom,
R earing the newborn lambs,
I maginative children playing in green fields,
N ice yellow daffodils,
G reen blades of fresh grass.

S unny sandy beaches,
U mbrellas put away,
M unching fresh strawberries,
M ilkshakes spilt down summer dresses,
E yes covered by sunglasses,
R ides on donkeys at the seaside.

A ll the leaves falling off the trees,
U nder the fallen leaves hedgehogs lay,
T ummies full of delicious foods,
U gly ducklings born,
M uddy wellies from muddy puddle jumping,
N ewborn babies snuggled up in fluffy blankets!

W ellies freezing from the snow,
I n Santa's grottos there's fluffy snow,
N ight-time falls early on,
T winkling fairylights glittering away,
E arly in the morning you wake up to pattering snow,
R ippling waves of white snow covering the pavement!

Abbie Myers (11)
Manor CE School, York

Go To Sleep

Go to sleep, Mum,
I won't go to sleep and not wake
Up, in the night.

Go to sleep, I won't
Break my cot bars and
Escape out the house.

Mum, I won't drink
The medicine the doctors gave Dad or
Stick a fork in a
Toaster, just go to sleep.

I won't cry
When you leave me with Nan:
I'll be happy playing with toys
I will be fine.

Sleep, Mum, sleep.
I won't
Try to climb a tree, play with your lighter,
Run across the highway or even think
About eating off the floor.

No, I won't
Make you embarrassed in front of friends,
Not like some.

I won't take drugs,
Get bad grades in my GCSE exams,
Get myself bullied
Or bully other kids.
I'll work well and get into university
And get a really ambitious job.

I promise, go to sleep,
I'll never forget
To ring you, email you, drop in
And if
I need a hug, I'll yell.

Hannah Barnett (12)
Manor CE School, York

The Antelope

The antelope
Cantering across the plain
His beauty overlooked
His potential underestimated
His skills unseen
He goes unnoticed
Unappreciated

Like my people
No one notices
Our potential
Or our skill
To them
We are all the same
Like a herd of antelope
Seen as a group
Instead of
Individuals

They don't bother
To get to know us
They don't see
That we're all
Unique

And as we pass unnoticed
Like thieves in the dead of night
Like a herd of antelope
Cantering across the plain
Overlooked
Underestimated
Unseen.

Ellie Griffin (13)
Manor CE School, York

Roads

Inspired by 'Nettles' by Vernon Scannell)

My son aged four got run down by a JCB,
Made for picking up things not putting them down,
He was mashed, mangled and mauled and laid in the mud,
Screams of pain echoed through the air,
JCBs are meant to be yellow not red,
I went out to see what was left,
But to my dismay I couldn't see much,
I tore out my phone and hit 999
I fumbled with my phone while it dialled,
The ambulance came within minutes,
And they were not ready for the shock,
While the JCB was nowhere to be seen,
They dragged him off the curb side and slung him on a trolley
It started to rain and his wounds were uncovered,
It was clear rain although the puddles were red,
The trolley was rammed into the ambulance and the doors slammed shut,
Unlucky for him now he won't be able to run into the road again,
I went to see him in hospital, he gave me a weak grin,
He didn't look too good,
The doctor said it had gone well on all the operations,
They said it would be a fair few weeks before he would be able
To come home but he would always have a handicap for the rest of his life,
It cost us a lot but we didn't care about that,
They then made a pelican crossing next to our house,
Pity it was a bit too late,
The JCB driver got two years in prison,
But I will never think that it was enough,
My child was traumatised,
It seemed to hurt him more on the inside than it did on the outside
But in years to come he did end up healing but he is left with the memories.

Joe Pollock (12)
Manor CE School, York

The Whales

The beaming sun shines down,
Waves race to the shore,
Fizzing the golden sand,
As the surface of the water shimmers.

Everything is perfect,
In my beautiful underwater kingdom,
Fellow fish greet me,
But some dart into the coral.

A plethora of minuscule fish,
All colours of the rainbow say 'hi',
A peaceful atmosphere,
But then Man came.

A long line of blood streams in front of my eyes,
Suddenly a call for help,
My brother's in trouble,
I stare at the bottom of the floating boat.

He helplessly lies next to it,
Bare hands pulling him onboard,
No more shriek for help,
Nothing.

A nearby friend told me,
How his razor sharp teeth snapped at them,
And how his colossal tail splashed them,
Breaking the calm surface.

So next time you see us,
If you get the chance,
Don't be like the men on that boat,
Instead just admire me and my friends, the whales.

Aimee Metcalfe (12)
Manor CE School, York

My Poem

Catherine of Aragon was a pain,
She was boring, maybe even plain.
She had a daughter named Mary,
She may have been a little hairy.
He married Catherine then felt remorse,
He created his own church then he got a divorce.

Anne Boleyn was very young,
Even though she never had a son,
She had a daughter named Lizzie,
Even when she was a baby she was always busy.
Anne filled Henry full of dread,
So he went and chopped off her head.

Jane Seymour was very gentle,
Even though she was a little mental,
She had a son named Ed,
Next thing you know she is falling dead.

Anne of Cleves was serious,
And she went a bit delirious,
Henry thought she looked like a horse,
It was time for another divorce.

Catherine Howard was very flirty,
And she didn't like getting dirty.
She also went to spy,
So now she had to go and die.

Catherine Parr was a nurse,
She was always a little terse.
She outlived Henry by a mile,
I bet all the Tudors wanted to smile.

Megan Lea (12)
Manor CE School, York

The Dark Figure

The dark figure will always be there when someone is swallowed from life
He sucks you dry from everything you had
And says he needs pay
For his non-existent wife

The blade he carries he does not use
He just has it for effect
He's never been known to die or to lose
To be beat or to be decked

If you dare to step inside
His workshop, you'll see
That it's filled with clocks and sunglasses
All hidden under lock and key

Normal, you can say, look some
But if you look carefully, you can see
The inscription on each one

Nobody has ever lived to tell the tale
Of what or who the words say
And if you ever see him doing his work
He'll cock his head and make you pay;
'When's it your turn? Let me see'.
'Your name, please do tell me'.

And for the rest of your life
You will find
That you ask the same question
In your mind
'When's it your turn? Let me see'.
'Your name, please do tell me'.

Bethany Fairburn (12)
Manor CE School, York

Bellum Solus Mortem Importat

(Inspired by 'Dulce Et Decorum Est' by Wilfred Owen)

The thud of our heavy, stubborn boots,
As they pound against the ground,
Like a sea of death,
Oblivious to taunting hoots.
Pain jolts through us with every step, with every sound.
Bullets whizz past us, deafening our ears,
Whilst planes fly above,
And we know the end nears
As the graceful doves swoop down bringing no mercy, no love.

Quickly! Quickly! There are bombs overhead!
We run the pain blood-curdling, sick,
While my friend finds his deathbed,
And away his last moments tick.
My eyes sting as I weep for his loss,
After all my pain, none is greater than this.
Into a wagon he is tossed,
His angels swoop down, and by my nightmare I am kissed.

What if it was you stood there?
Knowing your chances of living were low,
You'd been tempted into the lion's lair,
But now the cracks begin to show.
Your spirits would not be so high;
Your words would not be so pat,
As I say this is no lie,
Bellum Solus Mortem Importat.*

*War brings only death.

Rosalind Grace Harper (13)
Manor CE School, York

Without You

(Inspired by 'Without You' by Adrian Henri)

Without You my family would fight, argue and cry.
Without You chocolate would never be seen again.
Without You my home would vanish and I would be left in complete darkness
Without You make-up would make me ugly.
Without You my guinea pig would be homeless and lonely.
Without You friends would bully me every day.
Without You the iPod touch wouldn't have the touch.
Without You food wouldn't help the hungry.
Without You shopping would be illegal.
Without You people wouldn't smile or laugh.
Without You my feet wouldn't pick up the beat of the Samba.
Without You people would die before they were even born.
Without You there would be
no daytime,
no butterflies,
no good music,
no toys to cuddle at night,
no trees,
no animals,
no weather,
no children,
no bedtime stories,
no laughter,
no education,
there'd be no freedom in this world
Without You.

Brittany Lowe (12)
Manor CE School, York

War

World War One
Invented the gun
Shooting started
Never to stop.

World War Two
Was a waste of time
Hitler was not a nice man.
It started when one guy shot another
Then the people watching attacked.

Tony Blair
Took us to war
Then the protesters walked.
Walking down
The streets and towns
For their rightful say
About the war.

Gordon Brown
Hoped to help a country
Against the Taliban.
Bullets flying
Death toll rising
In Afghanistan.

Countries drew soldiers back
For war is unnecessary.
My opinion is that war should be stopped
To save people dying.

Charlie Hosier (11)
Manor CE School, York

The River Cat

The river is a racing cat,
Thundering through the land.

The river cat's fur,
Is sleek and brown.

She tickles the large trees,
Just how she sharpens her claws.

Sometimes loud, sometimes quiet,
And never makes a sound.

As she hunts through the valley,
And prowls through the undergrowth.

She is looking for a path,
Which way shall she go?

The whistling wind howls
To the river cat.

In the darkness of night,
She captures the moonlight,
In her grasp.

She purrs.
She howls.

And when people hear her rippling sound, people say
'Oh no, it's the river cat.'

Katy Woodall (12)
Manor CE School, York

The Seasons

Seasons,
Times of the year,
All of the seasons are,
Winter, spring, summer, autumn,
That's them.

Winter is so cold,
Snow just showers over York,
At least it's Christmas.

Springtime is the best,
It's like rain of happiness,
Wait until next year.

Summer is awesome,
It is hours of sunshine,
But not in Yorkshire.

Autumn is so wet,
Like God sneezing over us,
Bless you God, bless you.

Seasons,
Times of the year,
All of the seasons are,
Winter, spring, summer, autumn,
That's them.

Alexander Nicholas Scadding (11)
Manor CE School, York

The Predator

Your humanity erased from first bite.
Icy skin now feels the rain not sun.
Senses and emotions enhanced for your hunt.
The craving will never leave you.
Not till a stake slows your heart.

Sophie Windass (15)
Manor CE School, York

Seasons

Summer
The burning sun
Fiery, warming me
Though I get burnt and go in
Such pity

Autumn
Coppery tones
First frost on fallen leaves
Showers of red, gold and orange
Peaceful

Winter
Snowflakes settle
The ground covered in frost
Leafless trees like gnarled skeletons
Lifeless

Spring comes
Life now blossoms
Beauty, everywhere
Life, walking, crawling and flying
Lovely.

Zach Brown (11)
Manor CE School, York

Day And Night

The sun rises, the stars are shining,
At the crack of dawn, the boy goes to sleep,
The postman is doing his morning rounds, as the last car comes home,
The boy gets dressed as he goes to bed,
Getting his breakfast, dreaming sweet dreams,
Getting in the car and having his dinner,
In his lessons, leaving his school.

Alastair Oliver (11)
Manor CE School, York

Without You

(Inspired by 'Without You' by Adrian Henri)

Without you it would be like having a family with no mother,
Without you it would be like having a group of friends who just always leave you out,
Without you life would be disappointing just like when you log onto Facebook and have no notifications,
Without you life is like a school corridor during lessons - empty,
Without you it is like when your favourite song comes on your ipod and it runs out of battery halfway through it,
Without you it is like you sleep however you don't remember your dream,
Without you it is like eating chicken nuggets without chips,
Without you it is like having a conversation without any words,
Without you it is like looking at a wardrobe and thinking *I have nothing to wear*,
Without you it is like when you can't find your door keys in the pouring down rain,
Without you it is like when you can't perfect your gymnastics routine days before the championships,
Without you there would be
No Topshop, no Republic, no Primark
No love, no hope, no faith
No feelings, no desire, no ambitions
There would be no rights or fairness
Without you.

Nancy McPeake (13)
Manor CE School, York

As I Lie Here Waiting

As I lie here waiting,
I think of all the things I could have done,
What could have been lost,
What could have been won,

But now I know what's coming,
I know what will happen,
As the feeling seeps in,
And my heart starts drumming,

As I lie here waiting,
I remember that no one can help me,
No one can hear my pain or grief,
And no one can see how I knew I was dying,

And suddenly there is a knock on my window,
Wait, more like a tap than a knock,
A gentle noise that left an angel,
An angel of incredible flawlessness coming for me,

As I lie here waiting,
The angel wisps over and lets me dream,
All I see is a bright light that burns my eyes,
But soon it dims and begins to be a gleam,
And then I'm peaceful and it all turns dark,
As I lay there waiting.

Katie Drummond (12)
Manor CE School, York

Without You

(Inspired by 'Without You' by Adrian Henri)

Without you the sun wouldn't rise
And we would have to live every day in darkness.
Without you Liverpool FC and Everton FC would be friends.
Without you being hugged by my mum
Would feel like I was being squashed by a bear.
Without you the only toppings available on
A pizza would be Brussel sprouts.
Without you the stars would run out of shine.
Without you I would have all my
Family and friends taken off me.
Without you Santa would take instead of give.
Without you watching football would feel like watching golf.
Without you every night 'The Simpsons' would
Be cancelled and 'Bargain Hunt' would take its place.
Without you my heart would be starved of love.
Without you
There'd be no water in the sea, no sand on beaches,
No seasons, no life.
There'd be no sun, no moon, no universe,
Without you.

Rakib Uddin (13)
Manor CE School, York

Stuff I Like Matters To Me

Sometimes I get lost in a world full of information
Sometimes I just get lost
The teachers are like Looney Tunes
School dinners are lovely, it's like being in Heaven.

I like Wales' rugby team, they are legends
They are like a bulldozer coming towards you.

Declan Daniel (11)
Manor CE School, York

Scribbles

Scribbles, scribbles used everywhere
In birthday cards
And pictures of hair.

Without scribbles no one would write
Children wouldn't learn,
The pages would be white.

Scribbles, scribbles used everywhere
Writing draughts
And clouds in the air.

Without scribbles no stories would be written
No scripts; no films
No cream when you are bitten.

Scribbles, scribbles used everywhere
This is what matters to me
Health and safety warnings are a matter of care.

The rules and laws
Are written for a cause
All made because of scribbles.

Evelyn Allison (12)
Manor CE School, York

Xbox

My Xbox games
The games are
Like
Black Ops
With the
Excitement
And horror
And
Blood.

Connor Garnett (11)
Manor CE School, York

Happiness

Do you know how I feel when I wake up, roll over and look into your eyes?
When I feel your warm breath upon my neck?
When I feel your soft hands clinging to my waist?
It feels like happiness.
Happiness is like a warm cup of tea on the coldest morning,
Happiness is a gleaming ocean on the darkest night,
Happiness is the most beautiful sunset on the worst day.
Happiness is you and me forever . . .
You're the first thing I see on a morning and the last thing I see on a night,
Until the end you are my special happiness.
And there is no one else, no other way, I would rather spend my day with you,
There is nothing anyone can do to stop me loving you,
They can tell lies,
They can break my arms and legs,
There is nothing,
We'll last forever.
So when the end is near,
I will have no fear,
Because when time stops and there are no more clocks,
Our time ticks on forever more . . .

Kiera Brookes (13)
Manor CE School, York

Without You

(Inspired by 'Without You' by Adrian Henri)

Without you every day is a rainy day,
Without you chocolate would taste like cardboard,
Dry and tasteless.
Without you a rainbow would be a hurricane,
Wet, wild and windy.
Without you it would always be night,
Dark and dull.
Without you perfect dreams would become terrifying nightmares.
Without you the sun will go on vacation and never come back again.
Without you there would be no movies at the cinema.
Without you I would never be whole ever again,
Always with a piece of my heart missing.
Without you all the daisies in the world would wilt and die,
There would be no poppy fields.
Without you there would be
No sandwiches and no KitKats
No picnics on the beach and no paddling in the sea
or burying people in the sand.
That's what the world would be like *without you.*

Daisy Pitchers (12)
Manor CE School, York

Without You

(Inspired by 'Without You' by Adrian Henri)

Without you bad hair days would be part of everyday life.
Without you bubblegum would just be regular gum.
Without you World War II would have never ended.
Without you rosy red poppies would be colourless.
Without you luxury hand soap would be Tesco's value hand soap.
Without you every day would be a natural disaster.
Without you there would be no springs on trampolines.
Without you winter would last all year round.
Without you feelings would be non-existent.
Without you love would be a dream, never reality.
Without you Pot Noodles would just be empty pots.
Without you the Nike tick would be a cross instead.
Without you life wouldn't be worth living.
Without you there would be;
No school, no forgiveness, no love,
No friends, no ice cream van at the end of school, no hope,
No laughter, no kindness, no sand on beaches,
No moon, no sun, no clouds, no life
Without you!

Keely Horne (13)
Manor CE School, York

Dulce Et Decorum Est 2010

Sent to defend the rights of a country
That will not remember them but for
One day in the winter gloom where all
Of Helmand were awoken by an almighty
Boom, the heat and dust obscure from sight
As all of Britain asks the same question
Is this a winnable fight?
Helmand bears the blood of the Guards, Rifles and
Marines, killed by the hidden Devil of IEDs.
As they fight hidden in trees our brave
Soldiers fight back with their rifles and smgs
Ill-equipped, lowly paid as their families wait all worried and afraid
No more do we fight face to face, yet still
Entangled in a giant arms race.
Solemnly Afghan, Taliban and Mujhadin all laugh
At Western politicians, who talk, posture and lie
While soldiers no longer unknown die by the score.
Flown home in bags in the back of a plane
Needing to believe the immortal lie
'Dulce et decorum est pro patri a mori.'

Joseph Lawson (12)
Manor CE School, York

The Battle Of Battles

(Inspired by 'Dulce Et Decorum Est' by Wilfred Owen)

Slipping over, like on a dirty ice-rink,
Bloody, bruised, coughing like smokers
As we wandered through the murky graveyard,
'Til we reached the haunting, hunched trenches where
We crouched hastily, facing our deranged enemies.
Smoking shots were fired. Comrades bled lakes
But continued the battle.
We were all dead men,
When the bullets ripped the air.

Watch out! The cry of a wounded animal,
As we hid behind the lanky trenches;
And before our sleepless eyes I saw him
Falling, flailing as red liquid poured out
Of his rigid, dirty body.
Caught, hand in hand with death,
We watched him fall to the afterlife.

All my nightmares had come to me,
As my beloved brother lay still, silent and sorrowful.

Callum Dunnington (13)
Manor CE School, York

My Version Of Dulce Et Decorum Est

(Inspired by 'Dulce Et Decorum Est' by Wilfred Owen)

Legs-bent, like a little kid looking for a lost toy,
Backs-braced, coughing like hags,
We swore through bloody-mud,
Till we stopped and another fell, this time a boy,
The bullet pierced his heart, and then came the blood,
Broken bones wail in terror. Arms stained with sludgy blood,
And sleepy soldiers stumbled forwards, their thoughts of warmth turned to trudge,
Their shoes soon to be turned to tattered cords.

Run! Run! Quick boys! An ecstasy of stumbling,
As the shells started to rain down;
But someone was still tripping and lumbering,
And mist swirled around him, surrounding him, like a deathly grey gown . . .
And through the foggy gas I saw a shapeless lump fall to the graveyard of a field.

In all my nightmares, before my scarred sight, I saw the mist fall around him in shocked silence as his eyes were drained from all life,
Bleeding. Dying . . . Dead.

Emily Croxson (13)
Manor CE School, York

City At Night

The car sprints on the floor.
The sewers cry for all their life.
Streetlights look down at me angrily.
The train goes to sleep at the train station.

The houses watch me all night long.
The telly is seeing all channels at the same time.

The trees speak but I cannot hear.
All the balls jump along hitting me in my back.

Will this madness ever end?
Moons watch me madly.
Brushes have spoken to me.
The wind shouts in my ear.
Pathways hide to block me.
Gateways look at me like I am nothing.

Will the hatred stop at me?
Greedy walls keep trying to push me around.
Bikes run at me but stop at the stairs.
Bins smash into me.
All the bad things come to an end but it will return.
And I will be ready.

Jack Warren (12)
Manor CE School, York

Fifth Floor

Sweetheart, I think you'd better
Turn on the television
Turn on the television
Daddy's famous

He'll be home soon
And we can all relax
We can breathe easy
He's on the fifth floor

His voice sweetened my ear
Earlier today
He lit up my room with his laugh
Don't worry, he shan't be long

The plane hit the building
The top floor demolished
But he's on the fifth floor
He'll be back soon

Sweetheart, I think you'd better
Turn on the television
Turn on the television
To watch Daddy die.

Eliza Phillips (15)
Manor CE School, York

What Matters To You?

Immigration matters to me!

Their rights
In their own home
They are getting abused
Persecuted in their country
Save them!

Escape
Scared and frightened
They only want to leave
To be able to live safely
Let them!

New chance of life:

New life
To live in hope
They only want one chance
What have they ever done to you?
Come on!

Tom Boorman (11)
Manor CE School, York

Nature Poem

Winter is here, the air is cold
The year is ending and growing old.
The frost is here, it bites my face
Now it's time to slow my pace.
The snow is crunching as I walk
I see my breath when I talk.
Icicles hang up above
And frosty rooftops which I love.

Nature, nature all around
Heaven is here in the nature I've found.

Leah Craine (12)
Manor CE School, York

Nature Matters To Me

Blossom,
A striking scene,
Magical fairy dust,
Floating down to greet the damp grass,
Blossom,

A stream,
Trickling down,
A peaceful mess,
Swirling round the glistening trees,
Twirling,

The sun,
Alive and round,
A static ball of life,
Glittering always on duty,
Happy.

Eleanor Brierley (12)
Manor CE School, York

The Wonderful World Of Nature

The moon is glowing,
The autumn trees are blowing,
Whilst the dawn birds sing,
Then it happens,
The sun glistens wildly,
Dew lies across the floor,
This frosty morn I awake again,
For the new day.

The sun,
Takes the moon's place,
In the sky joyfully,
Hopes the day will never end,
The sun.

Florence Croxson (11)
Manor CE School, York

Bovis No Incumbo (Bullets Fly Overhead)

(Inspired by 'Dulce Et Decorum Est' by Wilfred Owen)

Looking over like a child peeking over a wall.
Terrible trenches, bullets, flying like bees.
Dodging, ducking, avoiding the bullets, always on the ball.
They crawl through the bloody sludge,
Scraping their knees.
They slept as they walked,
Shoeless, not stopping and never resting.
They looked around to find where they were, they were clueless.
Until they saw the birds dead, meant to be resting.

Fire! Fire! Napalm hide! Running like a child.
Running from a monster in a terrible dream,
I lay by my father before he died, there were no words, he just smiled.
My dreams tore apart at the seams, I realised
I may have escaped the fire but what I had seen,
Was like a searing and burning pain in my heart.
But I knew no matter what war there is,
There will always be bovis no incumbo.

Calvin Laverick (13)
Manor CE School, York

Without You Poem

(Inspired by 'Without You' by Adrian Henri)

Without you the children in the Primark factories would get a fair pay.
Without you Whip-Ma-Whop-Gate would be the longest street in the world.
Without you I would be taller than Nancy and Ellie,
in fact the tallest in the world.
Without you water would taste and be the consistency of blood.
Without you at Christmas Santa wouldn't get stuck down our chimneys.
Without you I would take compliments as insults.
Without you there would be only 25 letters in the alphabet.
Without you no one would die of cancer.
Without you colouring pencils would be colourless.
Without you kids would never grow up.
Without you birds wouldn't be able to fly.
Without you a blind man would be able to see
and a deaf man would be able to hear.
Without you there would be . . .
No ice cream, no hands on clocks, square wheels on bikes,
no cars, no TVs.
Without you.

Mollie Salter (12)
Manor CE School, York

Dulce Et Decorum Est

(Inspired by 'Dulce Et Decorum Est' by Wilfred Owen)

Stranded on the battlefields like dogs I saw them.
Dying, drowning in a sea of gas gagging like their lungs were closing up.
Everywhere I looked bombshells were scattered,
Their bodies enveloped with blood and cuts.
Some silent soldier trudged across with a gun in his hand, ready to shoot, at his next victim.
The sound of shooting split the air.
I saw a body being carried in a wagon, how my heart broke.

'Help! Help!' I heard a young man pleading.
I sprinted over; he was clutching his heart in agonising pain.
I dragged him away while bullets continued to kill.
Blood dripped on his uniform making a crimson pool on the floor.
As I lay him on the battlefields, the colour drained from his face, leaving him as white as chalk.
As he lay motionless, dead, I sat up and wiped my forehead. As I gazed around.
The old lie: dulce et decorum est pro patria mori.

Naomi Halliday (13)
Manor CE School, York

The Last Monster

We are the village people marching together
With noise loud as thunder and swords at our side,
Through caves and over hills and cruel weather
To the forests in the mountains where the last monster hides.
We are the village people marching together
To challenge the terrible man-eating beast,
To catch it, to drag it back home and tether
So children need never to be afraid of monsters again.
We are the people marching.
I'm the last monster, waiting and old,
Shivering all day in the dark damp den I call home,
Life's not worth living anymore, everything is blurred,
Cramped in this dungeon of a cave as the fog swirls around.
I'm the last monster waiting and old,
Once I was feared, furious and bold,
Once my eyes glittered in the sun, but now everything's all blurred,
Nothing's more sad than a monster growing old and wrinkly.
I'm the last monster, waiting.

Liam Morgan (13)
Manor CE School, York

School

Inspired by 'Nettles' by Vernon Scannell)

My son aged five had his first day at school.
'First' seemed a funny word for such a day of dread,
That troop of scowling teachers and sniggering children:
It was no place for learning. The fright and sobs,
My boy came looking for friends and I saw
A hand push his tiny chest.
I soothed him till his neglect did not feel so painfully raw.
At last his eyes lit up and shone,
And then I prepared my words, disappointment and anger
And marched to the teacher, I complained in fury, slicing her with my tongue.
Till not a child in that brutal class
Dared taunt anymore. And then I warned,
Those teachers that it would never happen again,
But in just two weeks the falling outs and insults
Had grown a division in the small group of friends:
My son would often hit that stone cold floor again.

Bella McEvoy (12)
Manor CE School, York

Without You

(Inspired by 'Without You' by Adrian Henri)

Without you it would take an hour just to get to the shop and another hour to get back
Without you I couldn't watch 'The Simpsons'
Without you I would have an empty cage and no one to give my veg to
Without you when I go to sleep it would be like sleeping on a bed of nails
Without you the winters would be brutal
Without you I would be naked
Without you nothing would come through my earphones when I'm bored
Without you I could not go on msn
Without you the day would be dark
Without you my hair would be flat and it would feel like I was bald
Without you there would be
No friends, no family, no good times
No day, no night, no sunshine
No fields, no hills, no rivers
No fun, no happiness
Without you.

James Wright (12)
Manor CE School, York

I Am Grateful For . . .

My cat.
My cat is fiery, like the hazy beams of an African sunset,
Calm yet notable.
Fiery like the flash of flavour from a spicy pepperoni pizza,
Hot yet familiar,
Fiery like the blinding sight of the sun flooding through curtains every
Saturday morning, wild yet relaxing.
My cat is fearless.

He is like winter.
My cat is like a statue, common yet agile.
Cold and joyless, he is also graceful and sudden,
Like the surrender of leaves in the crispy autumn's shift.
My cat is like the laughter of my friends, playful and friendly,
My cat is bold, like the fearless adventures of tomorrow
Bold like endless meadows of emerald grass, regular yet different,
Bold like a hearty Sunday pub lunch.

It is my cat I am grateful for.

Olivia Gabraitis (13)
Manor CE School, York

Her Eyes Went Still

He looked coldly into my eyes,
His eyes went still.
I knew that all he said was lies,
His eyes went still.
He was my best mate,
His eyes went still.
The one which I grew to hate,
His eyes went still.
Little did I know he was sleeping with my wife,
His eyes went still.
She vowed to be mine, forever, for life,
His eyes went still.
I caught them in my bedroom, red-handed,
His eyes went still.
I snapped her neck, left him 'dead-handed',
Her eyes went still.

My wife - the cheater.

Joe Chapman (14)
Manor CE School, York

Without You

(Inspired by 'Without You' by Adrian Henri)

Without you friends would never return a favour,
Without you light would be as popular as sausage butties,
Without you drink would drown everyone,
Without you pets would become everyone's nightmare,
Without you in football there would be no objective.
Without you life wouldn't be worth living,
Without you Westminster would be St Paul's pizza parlour,
Without you family would be your worst enemies,
Without you Xbox would be like staring into a blank screen,
Without you sleep would be pointless,
Without you there would be,
No light, no chocolate, no burials,
No chip shops, no bakeries, no people in markets,
No dogs in kennels, no scent,
No sound, there'd be no city, no country, no town,
Without you.

Callum Crosby (13)
Manor CE School, York

What Matters To Me!

The world matters to me,
It's a beautiful place to be in,
There are millions of amazing animals you can see,
meet and find out about.
The world is a beautiful place to be in,
You can explore hundreds and thousands of fabulous cities and countries.
The world is a beautiful place to be in,
The world is full of lots of fabulous people to meet.
The world is a beautiful place to be in,
You can visit museums and there are loads of fabulous
and incredible places to see.
That is what really matters to me!

Mollie Yeomans (11)
Manor CE School, York

Without You

(In the style of 'Without You' by Adrian Henri)

Without you the world would be black and white.
Without you England would beat Germany at football.
Without you there would be no families.
Without you my Sunday roast beef would taste like sprouts.
Without you friends would be bullies.
Without you eating would make you hungry.
Without you not eating pancakes would be a crime punishable by a fine of £1000 and five months in jail.
Without you Spider-Man would not be able to shoot webs.
Without you people would be paid in pennies instead of pounds.

Without you there would be no lakes
No oceans, no wind, no towns
No money, no friends, no cars on motorways
No trees or plants, no life or people
There'd be no continents, no world.

Julian Denecke (12)
Manor CE School, York

First World War Poem

(Inspired by 'Dulce Et Decorum Est' by Wilfred Owen)

People crying, like newborn babies,
The gas tore us apart in seconds,
The sound of people crying faded into the wind,
With an everlasting fog that grew and grew,
The pain cried out with screeches.

'Help! Help! I need some help over here,'
Filling the night sky with sorrow and despair,
There he was, dying in the wind,
The night sky was filled with bloodshed, how many more?
The mist and thick fog rose up and I heard,
Cries of death that echoed into the breeze . . .

Robert Hand (13)
Manor CE School, York

Just Screaming

(Inspired by 'Dulce Et Decorum Est' by Wilfred Owen)

Bent and crooked, like invalid men without sticks,
Stumbling-struggling, hobbling along like old age,
Bombs drop with a gentle kick,
We trudged along, forgetting the pain, like we were in a protective cage,
Bleeding backs scream, many have lost their wits,
But we crawled on. All cried shameful tears,
They endeavour to carry on, but gave up and he sits,
The gas shells drop, and all dash with fears.

Screaming! Screaming! All fumbling around,
Fitting the cruel helmets before the blow,
Cries came, 'Another' as the mist took its bond,
At a strangling crawl he fell from the third row,
To see him howl through the thick light,
As if the sky was falling, I saw his cries,
In all my nightmares I see him on that night,
The way he was screaming at me, where he lies.

Bethan Ward (13)
Manor CE School, York

Without You

(Inspired by 'Without You' by Adrian Henri)

Without you football wouldn't have a ball,
Without you when I play my Xbox I'd stare at a blank screen,
Without you Weightwatchers would be full of skinny people,
Without you today would be tomorrow and tomorrow would be today,
Without you no cars would have any petrol in,
Without you salt and vinegar would be vinegar and salt,
Without you the sun would be as dark as a black hole,
Without you every sofa would be bumpy,
Without you it would be school every day of the week
Without you every song would be a high pitched squeal,
Without you there would be no light,
Without you there would be no TV, no roads, no chip shops,
No beaches, no cinema, no arcades,
No parks, no light, no homes,
There'd be no fun, no happiness
Without you.

Dominic Kelsey-Crockett (12)
Manor CE School, York

The Pot Hole

Inspired by 'Nettles' by Vernon Scannell)

My son, aged 9, fell off his bike today.
An understatement 'fell' for those sharp grains of sand,
Those rough waves of pain on the way to school.
It was with swells of tears like salty seas
The boy came searching for safe harbour
I saw deep trenches filled by dark red blood.
At last he offered up a watery smile.
I hastily took up my first aid kit
Swept away blood and grit with fresh water
Till not a speck of gravel rash blemished his smooth skin.
Then I filled brim-full the hole.
But in two weeks harsh traffic's passage had
Emptied it out again -
A deep sea cave.
My son would often feel sharp wounds again.

David Clarke (12)
Manor CE School, York

Love

Every time I look,
My heart skips a beat,
It's like reading a good book,
When our lips meet,
It's like Heaven's own touch,
When you hold me,
I want more; so much,
To be near you is my life's goal,
You're the light of my dark,
The mate of my soul,
It's like a great walk in the park,
When I look into your eyes,
I feel a broken heart,
Please leave her for me,
Help me please,
Save me from this love disease.

Georgia Fearn (12)
Manor CE School, York

Wasps

Inspired by 'Nettles' by Vernon Scannell)

My son aged three got stung by a wasp.
'Stung' seemed a curious word for those mini missiles,
The swarm of soldiers in their base
It was no place to rest, with sobs and tears
The boy came looking for comfort and I saw
The shining missile sticking from his arm
I soothed him until it no longer hurt
At last he offered me a weeping smile
And then outside I went and shook the spray
And killed all the wasps until not a
Single one remained and then I lit
The funeral pyre to burn the fallen dead.
But in two weeks of sun and rain
The wasps were back again
My son would feel the sharp pain again.

David Stanton (13)
Manor CE School, York

One And Only King Of Pop

His name was Michael Joseph Jackson loved worldwide,
He started singing young with his brothers by his side,
Jackie, Tito, Jermaine, Marlon and of course Michael lead,
We never can say goodbye to him such a powerful seed,
He taught us a lot, ABCs, 123s and Ben was a special rat,
And we loved this music with him as he grew just like that,
He sang I'll Be There and in our hearts he was right there,
He sang his other songs like Bad, Can You Feel It
And come to love him everybody from everywhere,
At times he was at odds with himself with songs like Scream,
Leave Me Alone and Childhood
The king of pop has been surely misunderstood,
But then he came back strong with Thriller and Beat It,
And as we sang these songs
Mimicking Michael Jackson's dancing in our living room
We knew the king of pop could never be defeated.

Chloe Dudley (13)
Manor CE School, York

Thorn Bush

Inspired by 'Nettles' by Vernon Scannell)

My daughter aged five fell in a thorn bush.
'Bush' seemed the wrong name for those sharp spikes,
That patch of hate in the woods:
It was no place to sleep, with blood and tears.
The girl came looking for her mum and saw
Deep cuts slit in her tender skin.
I soothed her and cleaned her cuts.
At last she showed us her brilliant smile,
And then I took my hedge clippers, and a bin
And went to the woods and cut those thorns away
Till not one thorn lay on the ground dangerous anymore.
And then I took them to the trash and threw them in,
But after spring when the weather and
Heat grew the thorns back up in the woods:
My daughter will get bloody wounds again.

Amber Snowden (12)
Manor CE School, York

My Home

Home is like the kindness of my mum;
Safe, protective, helping me fly.
Home means as much as the sun,
Glowing red in a sunset sky.
Home is still as fun as my brother,
Always there, making me laugh!
Home is made of individual strands,
Coming together. The perfect scarf.
Home makes me think of my grandparents,
Always there, but sometimes far away.
Whether my home is messy or tidy,
Whatever the weather, I want to stay.
Home shows the strength of my dad;
There forever, making me stronger.
My home is there even when I'm sad,
But my family's there even longer.

Jennifer Moulds (14)
Manor CE School, York

Injections

Inspired by 'Nettles' by Vernon Scannell)

My daughter aged five had to have a jab,
'Jab' seemed an unusual name for that painful stinging needle,
That harsh grenade lurking at the hospital:
It was no peaceful haven. With worrying and anxiety
The girl showed me and I told her to smile
While the angry zit on her arm throbbed more.
Finally her tears stopped after a while
Then I seized the medicine
And gave it to her
An d there was no more gore.
And then I said a last goodbye
To the dead, empty missile,
She would keep feeling so much pain.
And as my daughter was feeling so vile
We were seeing the doctor again.

Zara Thewlis (12)
Manor CE School, York

Doctors

Inspired by 'Nettles' by Vernon Scannell)

My son aged three had his first trip to the doctors.
'Trip' seemed a strange name like going somewhere fun,
It was this horrible adventure:
No place of comfort for little boys. Trembling and screaming
The boy came seeking comfort and I saw
How frightened he really was.
I calmed him till he was not screaming.
At last he gave us a little smile,
And then I took, his trembling hand
And went outside away from the pain.
Till not a bit of that horrible place was in sight. And then I bought
Him his favourite sweets,
But in two weeks the busy chill and rain
Had made us go back to the dreaded place:
My son would often feel that tremor again.

Natalie Knowles (12)
Manor CE School, York

Death

Inspired by 'Nettles' by Vernon Scannell)

My daughter aged 12 was laid to rest.
'Rest' seemed a strange name for the grasp of death,
That bony hand of the Grim Reaper, black he is dressed:
It is not time for sleep.
With charts and graphs the doctors came and told me she would slip away.
We told her too and comforted her until she understood,
'Maybe I'm saving a baby's life,' she said.
At last I chose a coffin, one that she would like
And I laid her in it,
Till the soft silk held her delicate body.
And then I crossed her arms and in her hand I placed a flower,
But in two days her friends and family gathered with me and
We put our gloved hands together as we cried:
My daughter would never feel hurt again.

Louisa Rayner (12)
Manor CE School, York

The Eagle

Death sweeps through the valley like the majestic eagle.
His knife-like beak dripping with blood.
His eyes staring into my very soul.
With every swipe of his huge wings disease sprays on the closest to him.
He has death defying speed, you can't run away.
He has the strength to snap you in half like a twig.
You cannot hear him but you can feel his presence like ice on a frozen morning.
His feathers are long and sharp like the spikes on a cactus.
He can tear you apart like the air we walk through.
His ear deafening squawk pierces the silence so you can no longer hear.
Life has no meaning to this fearsome creature.
Death is all he knows.
He uses precise movements like the stitch of a wound.

Dillon Thompson (12)
Manor CE School, York

Nettles

Inspired by 'Nettles' by Vernon Scannell)

My sister aged five fell in the playground.
'Playground' seemed a curious name for that obstacle of people,
That bruises and cuts behind the school's benches;
It was no place for play. With sobs and tears
The girl told me at home seeking comfort and I saw
A large cut carved in her delicate skin.
I soothed her and told her it would be alright.
At last she offered me a little smile,
As then I took my brush, from the pantry
And went outside and in fury making sure all loose
Tarmac was out the way. And then I made sure
There was no more there to trip and fall.
But then in two weeks the busy children would soon kick
The tarmac and there would be wounds again.

Estella Mackenzie (12)
Manor CE School, York

Never Gone

Now the pain has subsided, there's a hole in my heart.
Each time I think of you and how you enlightened my life,
My heart yearns for you to hold me again.
I miss how you used to hold me when I was sad
and how you'd wipe away my tears when I cried.
You've gone and left me alone in the dark.
Why did you leave before I had the chance to say goodbye?
It was you I cried for when you left that night.
The night you died. A piece of me died with you.
I've realised now that I can't change the fact that you're gone.
But to me you will always be alive in those who you cared about
And those who cared about you.
Family is forever and with each day that passes
is another day we will again be reunited.

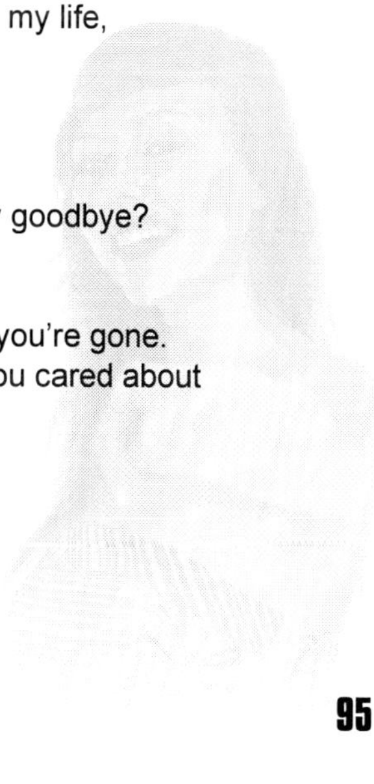

Loren Mackenzie (15)
Manor CE School, York

Dulce Et Decorum Est

(Inspired by 'Dulce Et Decorum Est' by Wilfred Owen)

Crouched, like old men in the gutter,
Grasping fingers clawed the dampened earth.
Shredded limbs weighed the tiresome men down.
Lulling them into a false sense of security.
The bullets whispered like ghosts through the air,
Taunting the little boys playing soldier,
The icy wind biting at their raw feet.

Soldiers danced across the field, God's fearless angels,
One by one, falling like birds pierced by the hunter.
Gas intoxicating their bodies, drowning in air,
Sweet, as the very froth that rumbled in their lungs.
Whoever could inflict this bitter fury should taste
The bloodshed by the brave for themselves.

Emma Darbyshire (13)
Manor CE School, York

Rugby

Inspired by 'Nettles' by Vernon Scannell)

My son aged eight got tackled in a game of rugby,
'Game' seemed a weird name for such a violent sport.
That dreaded muddy pitch across the road,
It was no place for standing still, people diving in from all directions.
The boy came limping towards me, clutching his arm and leg,
Closer up I noticed cuts, bruises and scratches all over him.
I sat down and inspected his body, I could see his agony,
I cleaned up his wounds with water and tissues.
After a while he lifted himself up and gave me a warm hug,
Then I grabbed his arms and legs,
And carried him towards our house and forbid him to play rugby forever.
But in a month or so, he moved onto another sport, boxing.
He would often feel pain again!

Ben Whitehead (12)
Manor CE School, York

The Cold

Inspired by 'Nettles' by Vernon Scannell)

My brother aged three caught a cold.
'Caught' seems a curious word to go with that word of pain and misery.
It is usually associated with catch or ball games.
It was no place for rest, we had to get out of the life shortening cold.
With numb bums and aching legs he ran inside and hid under the cushion on the sofa.
His skin was paper white.
He was in bed until he wasn't so cold.
At last he got up and gave us a shivery smile.
Then I took my screwdriver and took off the lid of the boiler and went to work with the screwdriver.
Twisting and turning until my hands were red raw.
My brother now plays outside again but I know it will be similar next winter.

Jacob Schofield (13)
Manor CE School, York

Without You!

(Inspired by 'Without You' by Adrian Henri)

Without you there would be no S in M&S.
Without you every day would be a Wednesday with no end to the week.
Without you my birthday would be so boring I would fall asleep.
Without you Christmas would be like hell.
Without you colours would bleed into each other,
Turning the world a dull, dull grey.

Without you my favourite place would be gone forever.
Without you the Green Tree pub would be like any other pub I know.
Without you all the rivers would overflow and drown the world.
Without you there would be no cats, no dogs,
no horses, no ponies, no animals at all.
Nothing at all in our little world.

Jess Peacock (12)
Manor CE School, York

What Matters To Me?

Football matters to me!

The thrill of being there,
The hot dogs melting in my mouth,
Fans cheering all around the stadium,
Brilliant footwork and what a shot,
Oh, that was so close,
When will we score?
Oh no, they have got a chance!
What an acrobatic save!
We have got a chance,
He has weaved his way in and out,
Smacked his foot and in.
Goooaall!

Thomas McCrory (11)
Manor CE School, York

Technology

Technology's there as a symbol of hope.
Clicking and searching all over the web.
As you're doing your homework, before you go to bed.
The TV's there to watch The Fresh Prince of Bel Air.
Or sitting down with a cup of tea to watch Coronation Street.
Now going to Apple, it's not what you think.
You don't eat it or beat it.
You tweet on it and you live off it.
Xbox is there to wipe out PlayStation.
Bringing peace to Halo and Fable through the television.
Now military defence systems, they're funny things you know
But you don't want to press the red button.
Booooom!

Daniel Booth (13)
Ripon College, Ripon

Us Teenagers

After you read this nothing will be as it seems
About us teens

It's lies that you read in the mail
Cos they only have one side of the tale
About us teens

You'd think that we all smoke and drink
But the press really need to think
About us teens

You'd think that we always get into trouble
And that since we beat everyone up, we should carry a shovel
Us teens

You'd think that we all speak chav
And that nothing is all we'll ever have
Us teens

You'd think that all we ever do is punch and kick
But not all of us are really that thick
Us teens

You'd think that we all steal cash
That the only sound we know was smash
Us teens

The rich show their kids these things
And tell them to be grateful for living like kings
Us teens

You'd think we all wear hoodies to hide our face
And that we're all just a waste of space
Us teens

You'd think that we were all from the hood, you get me
And that we've never had a cup of tea
Us teens.

Becky Sheldon (13)
Ripon College, Ripon

What Matters To Me

My dog named Samantha
She used to be called Sam for short
It used to be me and her playing in the garden
But not anymore.

My dog Sam
I was born and I was filled with joy
To see lying on the sofa, a black glistening dog
I grew up with her and we had fun
Not one day was she not by my side
Well except from now and forever.

My dog Sam
She growled sometimes, or should I say most of the time
She would protect me whenever someone came up to me
She was glorious, my number one dog
I never wanted that day to come.

My dog Sam
One day when I woke up
I trotted downstairs, only to see Sam lying there not moving
I panicked and raced up to her
She was awake which brightened me up a bit
I opened the door to the garden, but she didn't move
She would normally charge out
She just looked up and looked back down again.

My dog Sam
I went to school thinking about Sam
I acted a bit stranger than normal
People asked me if I was okay
I came back home quickly
Only to find out Sam was leaving me forever
She was going to be put down.

My dog Sam
Mum said she was too old now and ill
So I went along with it
I realized she was ill because she couldn't move
She came back from the vets and I ran up crying
I sat there for at least an hour or two

Then my dad came to collect her
We buried her
We left some flowers on the grave

My dog Sam.

Chris Johnson (13)
Ripon College, Ripon

My Dog's Poem

My dog Woody is the greatest dog ever
He knows 'sit, lie down, roll over' and much more
He likes to chase cats
But I don't think he's chased bats
He's always on the move
But he needs manners to improve
He always tries to beg
But he only gets a rubber chicken leg
My dog Woody is my best friend
Until the world ends

My dog Woody has a little girlfriend
She is called Jessie, she is Woody's best friend
She can only so 'sit' and loves the smell of grit
She chews up shoes
And does loads of poos
She does a little wee
Then jumps with glee
She is very small, but jumps very high
Then she runs in the woods and doesn't say bye
She loves to sleep
But doesn't like cars when they beep
But what do you expect from a little girl?
She'll always be my little pearl.

Brandon Clarke (12)
Ripon College, Ripon

What Matters To Me

What matters to me
My great grandma
Each day I miss you more
Than ever
Today I think of all the
Memories
Walks to Studley,
Delicious lunches.

What matters to me
My great grandma
In my heart, and life
Forever
In my dreams each
Time I sleep
Memories of times together.

What matters to me
My great grandma
Served her life for our
Country
Driving vehicles, cooking
Meals
Using maps for directions.

What matters to me
My great grandma
Even after years have
Passed
You're always there
Beside me
But even though this poem's finished
You're always in my mind forever.

Charlotte Hillary (14)
Ripon College, Ripon

Love And Hate

She takes a glance in the mirror,
Her reflection say she's a quitter,
Not one could have said it better,
Or make her teardrops any wetter.

She combed her hair as if she'd care,
Her mind was lost between the lies,
Washed out faces and turned out cries.
Everything took her by surprise.

She took a breath,
One look said,
Crack a smile, let loose for a while,
So she said yes,
And made her mark all in red.

A brand new dress,
Made one to impress,
She met a man who asked for her hand,
And replied 'Yes, you can . . . '

She takes a glance in the mirror,
Her reflection says she is a quitter,
Not one could have said it better,
Or make her teardrops any wetter,

She combed her hair as if she'd care,
Her mind was lost between the lies
Washed out face turned out cries
No more lies,
No more cries, this girl was not a quitter
She just followed the category differ.

Ebony Lawson (14)
Ripon College, Ripon

My Animals

I love it when I cuddle up with my rabbits,
They keep me warm and are very fluffy,
I hate it when I have to clean my rabbits out,
They are very mucky and smelly,
I am a dog lover,
I love walking them,
I love playing with them,
I love my dog,
She is mine,
She is pretty,
She is like my best friend,
I love horses,
I love looking at them running around,
I used to go horse riding, till I fell off,
I don't love spiders,
They are creepy and crawly,
They are hairy,
I love cats,
But my mum will not let me have one,
They are cuddly and fluffy.

I love my animals
And they love me!

Lauren Styan (13)
Ripon College, Ripon

Shooting Stars

My friends and me are like shooting stars,
A bond so strong, it'll take us to Mars,
The fun times, the bad times, the high and the low,
We'll all stick together, wherever we go.

The times when we laugh uncontrollably loud,
The times when I feel unbelievably proud,
The times that we cry when we're all stressed out,
The times we fall out and we scream and shout.

My friends and me are like shooting stars,
A bond so strong, it'll take us to Mars,
The fun times, the bad times, the high and the low,
We'll all stick together, wherever we go.

The times when we talk for hours on end,
The times we got giddy and went round the bend,
The times we passed notes round the tables in school,
The times we thought we were 'just too cool'.

My friends and I are like shooting stars,
A bond so strong, it'll take us to Mars,
The fun times, the bad times, the high and the low,
I'll stay with my friends, wherever I go.

Alice Hoult (13)
Ripon College, Ripon

I Love My Cat!

I love my cat!
He makes my lap warm
He scratches on my door
He makes me feel loved
I love my cat!
He sits in the middle of my heart
He follows me all the way to the park
He crunches on his snacks
I love my cat!
He cuddles me when I'm sad
He was never so keen on my dad
He sometimes makes me mad but . . .
I love my cat!
He jumps up on my garden wall
He is ever so small
He only replies to Paul
I love my cat!
He never runs away
He sleeps by me day by day
He's always looking for me, even today
I love my cat!

Holly Attwater-Dunn (12)
Ripon College, Ripon

You Are Perfect!

If you were fat or skinny, it wouldn't matter to me,
You could be size zero or size thirty-three,
The colour doesn't matter of either your skin or your hair,
You could even be green - I really wouldn't care,
I would just look up or down, just to see your face,
And I would still smile if it was a disgrace,
So if you want to be my friend, you can count on me,
Because I'll still think you're perfect, no matter what I see!

Jasmine Leith (14)
Ripon College, Ripon

Featured Poets:
DEAD POETS
AKA Mark Grist & MC Mixy

Mark Grist and MC Mixy joined forces to become the 'Dead Poets' in 2008.

Since then Mark and Mixy have been challenging the preconceptions of poetry and hip hop across the country. As 'Dead Poets', they have performed in venues ranging from nightclubs to secondary schools; from festivals to formal dinners. They've appeared on Radio 6 Live with Steve Merchant, they've been on a national tour with Phrased and Confused and debuted their show at the 2010 Edinburgh Fringe, which was a huge success.

Both Mark and Mixy work on solo projects as well as working together as the 'Dead Poets'. Both have been Peterborough's Poet Laureate, with Mixy holding the title for 2010.

The 'Dead Poets' are available for workshops in your school as well as other events. Visit www.deadpoetry.co.uk for further information and to contact the guys!

Read on to pick up some fab writing tips!

Your WORKSHOPS

In these workshops we are going to look at writing styles and examine some literary techniques that the 'dead poets' use. Grab a pen, and let's go!

Rhythm Workshop

Rhythm in writing is like the beat in music. Rhythm is when certain words are produced more forcefully than others, and may be held for longer duration. The repetition of a pattern is what produces a 'rhythmic effect'. The word rhythm comes from the Greek meaning of 'measured motion'.

Count the number of syllables in your name. Then count the number of syllables in the following line, which you write in your notepad: 'My horse, my horse, will not eat grass'.

Now, highlight the longer sounding syllables and then the shorter sounding syllables in a different colour.

Di dum, di dum, di dum, di dum is a good way of summing this up.

You should then try to write your own lines that match this rhythm. You have one minute to see how many you can write!

Examples include:
'My cheese smells bad because it's hot'
and
'I do not like to write in rhyme'.

For your poem, why don't you try to play with the rhythm? Use only longer beats or shorter beats? Create your own beat and write your lines to this?

Did you know ... ?

Did you know that paper was invented in China around 105AD by Ts'ai Lun. The first English paper mill didn't open until 1590 and was in Dartford.

Rhyme Workshop

Start off with the phrase 'I'd rather be silver than gold' in your notepad. and see if you can come up with lines that rhyme with it -

'I'd rather have hair than be bald'
'I'd rather be young than be old'
'I'd rather be hot than cold'
'I'd rather be bought than sold'

Also, pick one of these words and see how many rhymes you can find:

Rose

Wall

Warm

Danger

What kinds of rhymes did you come up with? Are there differences in rhymes? Do some words rhyme more cleanly than others? Which do you prefer and why?

Lists Workshop

Game - you (and you can ask your friends or family too) to write as many reasons as possible for the following topics:

Annoying things about siblings

The worst pets ever

The most disgusting ingredients for a soup you can think of

Why not try writing a poem with the same first 2, 3 or 4 words?

I am ...

Or

I love it when ...

Eg:

I am a brother

I am a listener

I am a collector of secrets

I am a messer of bedrooms.

Onomatopoeia Workshop

Divide a sheet of A4 paper into 8 squares.

You then have thirty seconds to draw/write what could make the following sounds:

Splash	Ping
Drip	Bang
Rip	Croak
Crack	Splash

Now try writing your own ideas of onomatopoeia. Why might a writer include onomatopoeia in their writing?

Repetition Workshop

Come up with a list of words/ phrases, aim for at least 5. You now must include one of these words in your piece at least 6 times. You aren't allowed to place these words/ phrases at the beginning of any of the lines.

Suggested words/phrases:

Why

Freedom

Laughing

That was the best day ever

I can't find the door

I'm in trouble again

The best

Workshop POETRY 101

Below is a poem written especially for Poetry Matters, by MC Mixy.
Why not try and write some more poems of your own?

What is Matter?

© MC Mixy

What matters to me may not be the same things that matter to you
You may not agree with my opinion mentality or attitude
The order in which I line up my priorities to move
Choose to include my view and do what I do due to my mood
And state of mind
I make the time to place the lines on stacks of paper and binds
Concentrate on my artwork hard I can't just pass and scrape behind
Always keep close mates of mine that make things right
And even those who can't … just cos I love the way they can try
What matters to me is doing things the right way
It's tough this game of life we play what we think might stray from what others might say
In this world of individuality we all wanna bring originality
Live life and drift through casually but the vicious reality is
Creativity is unique
Opinions will always differ but if you figure you know the truth, speak
So many things matter to me depending on how tragically deep you wanna go
I know I need to defy gravity on this balance beam
As I laugh and breathe draft and read map the scene practise piece smash the beat and graphic release
Visual and vocal it's a standard procedure
Have to believe and don't bite the hand when it feeds ya

If you wanna be a leader you need to stay out of the pen where the sheep are
The things that matter to me are
My art and my friends
That will stay from the start to the end
People will do things you find hard to amend
Expect the attacks and prepare you gotta be smart to defend
I put my whole heart in the blend the mass is halved yet again
I'm marked by my pen a big fish fighting sharks of men
In a small pond
Dodging harpoons and nets hooks and predators tryna dismember ya
I won't let them I won't get disheartened I can fend for myself
As long as I'm doing what's important
I'm my mind where I'm supported is a just cause to be supporting
In these appalling hard times I often find myself falling when
Only two aspects of my life keep me sane and allow me to stand tall again
Out of all of them two is a small number
It's a reminder I remind ya to hold necessity and let luxury fall under
Try to avoid letting depression seep through
Take the lesson we actually need a lot less than we think we do
So what matters to you?
They may be similar to things that matter to me
I'm actually lacking the need of things I feel would help me to succeed
Though I like to keep it simple, I wanna love, I wanna breed
I'm one of many individuals in this world where importance fluctuates and varies
Things that matter will come and go
But the ones that stay for long enough must be worth keeping close
If you're not sure now don't watch it you'll know when you need to know
Me, I think I know now … yet I feel and fear I don't.

Turn overleaf for a poem by Mark Grist
and some fantastic hints and tips!

Workshop POETRY 101

What Tie Should I Wear Today?

© Mark Grist

I wish I had a tie that was suave and silk and slick,
One with flair, that's debonair and would enchant with just one flick,
Yeah, I'd like that … a tie that's hypnotizing,
I'd be very restrained and avoid womanising,
But all the lady teachers would still say 'Mr Grist your tie's so charming!'
As I cruise into their classrooms with it striking and disarming.
At parents' evenings my tie's charm would suffice,
In getting mums to whisper as they leave 'Your English teacher seems nice!'

Or maybe an evil-looking tie - one that's the business,
Where students will go 'Watch out! Mr Grist is
on the prowl with that evil tie.'
The one that cornered Josh and then ripped out his eye.
Yeah no one ever whispers, no one ever sniggers,
Or my tie would rear up and you'd wet your knickers.
Maybe one girl just hasn't heard the warning,
Cos she overslept and turned up late to school that morning,
And so I'd catch her in my lesson yawning … oh dear.
I'd try to calm it down, but this tie's got bad ideas.
It'd size the girl up and then just as she fears,
Dive in like a serpent snapping at her ears.
There'd be a scream, some blood and lots and lots of tears,
And she wouldn't be able to yawn again for years.

Or maybe … a tie that everyone agrees is mighty fine
And people travel from miles around to gawp at the design
I'd like that … a tie that pushes the boundaries of tieware right up to the limit
It'd make emos wipe their tears away while chavs say 'It's wicked innit?'
and footy lads would stop me with 'I'd wear that if I ever won the cup.'
And I'd walk through Peterborough to slapped backs, high fives, thumbs up
While monosyllabic teenagers would just stand there going 'Yup.'

I don't know. I'd never be sure which of the three to try
As any decision between them would always end a tie.

Tips and Advice for PERFORMING Your Poem

So you've written your poem, now how about performing it. Whether you read your poem for the first time in front of your class, school or strangers at an open mic event or poetry slam, these tips will help you make the best of your performance.

Breathe and try to relax.

Every poet that reads in front of people for the first time feels a bit nervous, when you're there you are in charge and nothing serious can go wrong.

People at poetry slams or readings are there to support the poets. They really are!

If you can learn your poem off by heart that is brilliant, however having a piece of paper or notebook with your work in is fine, though try not to hide behind these.

It's better to get some eye contact with the audience. If you're nervous find a friendly face to focus on.

Try to read slowly and clearly and enjoy your time in the spotlight.

Don't rush up to the microphone, make sure it's at the right height for you and if you need it adjusted ask one of the team around you.

Before you start, stand up as straight as you can and get your body as comfortable as you can and remember to hold your head up.

The microphone can only amplify what what's spoken into it; if you're very loud you might end up deafening people and if you only whisper or stand too far away you won't be heard.

When you say something before your poem, whether that's hello or just the title of your poem, try and have a listen to how loud you sound. If you're too quiet move closer to the microphone, if you're too loud move back a bit.

Remember to breathe! Don't try to say your poem so quickly you can't find time to catch your breath.

And finally, **enjoy!**

Poetry FACTS

Here are a selection of fascinating poetry facts!

No word in the English language rhymes with 'MONTH'.

William Shakespeare was born on 23rd April 1564 and died on 23rd April 1616.

The haiku is one of the shortest forms of poetic writing. Originating in Japan, a haiku poem is only seventeen syllables, typically broken down into three lines of five, seven and five syllables respectively.

The motto of the Globe Theatre was 'totus mundus agit histrionem' (the whole world is a playhouse).

The Children's Laureate award was an idea by Ted Hughes and Michael Morpurgo.

The 25th January each year is Burns' Night, an occasion in honour of Scotland's national poet Robert Burns.

Spike Milligan's 'On the Ning Nang Nong' was voted the UK's favourite comic poem in 1998.

Did you know *onomatopoeia* means the word you use sounds like the word you are describing – like the rain *pitter-patters* or the snow *crunches* under my foot.

'Go' is the shortest complete sentence in the English language.

Did you know rhymes were used in olden days to help people remember the news? Ring-o'-roses is about the Plague!

The Nursery Rhyme 'Old King Cole' is based on a real king and a real historical event. King Cole is supposed to have been an actual monarch of Britain who ruled around 200 A.D.

Edward Lear popularised the limerick with his poem 'The Owl and the Pussy-Cat'.

Lewis Carroll's poem 'The Jabberwocky' is written in nonsense style.

POEM – noun

1. a composition in verse, esp. one that is characterized by a highly developed artistic form and by the use of heightened language and rhythm to express an intensely imaginative interpretation of the subject.

Poetry TIPS

We have compiled some helpful tips for you budding poets...

In order to write poetry, read lots of poetry!

Keep a notebook with you at all times so you can write whenever (and wherever) inspiration strikes.

Every line of a poem should be important to the poem and interesting to read. A poem with only 3 great lines should be 3 lines long.

Use an online rhyming dictionary to improve your vocabulary.

Use free workshops and help sheets to learn new poetry styles.

Experiment with visual patterns - does your written poetry create a good pattern on the page?

Try to create pictures in the reader's mind - aim to fire the imagination.

Develop your voice. Become comfortable with how you write.

Listen to criticism, and try to learn from it, but don't live or die by it.

Say what you want to say, let the reader decide what it means.

Notice what makes other's poetry memorable. Capture it, mix it up and make it your own. (Don't copy other's work word for word!)

Go wild. Be funny. Be serious. Be whatever you want!

Grab hold of something you feel - anything you feel - and write it.

The more you write, the more you develop. Write poetry often.

Use your imagination, your own way of seeing.

Feel free to write a bad poem, it will develop your 'voice'.

Did you know ...?

'The Epic of Gilgamesh' was written thousands of years ago in Mesopotamia and is the oldest poem on record.

My Ginger Hair

Some may say it's a curse, not a blessing
But I think it's time to confess
That gingers are awesome
Not a pest

We're a dying breed
Desperately in need
But where would we be without gingers in the world?
And some might say they're annoying to be heard

But I think it's time to confess
That gingers are awesome
Not a pest

Like an Aryan race on the verge of extinction
We're a dying breed before our time
But my prediction is that we would have made it big time
Ruled the world like superstars
Sadly many would have us locked behind bars.

But I think it's time to confess
That gingers are awesome
Definitely not a pest.

Zak O'Brien (13)
Ripon College, Ripon

My Friends

My friends are all unique to me,
This will always be.
Our friendship was meant to be,
Just between them and me.

My friends are all so close to me,
They stick to me like glue.
Our bond is so tough,
Just between them and me.

Stacey Chandler (13)
Ripon College, Ripon

The Way It Is Now

All the thoughts, all the stress
I'm getting myself into a big mess
I don't need this, I really don't
I think I'm in a sinking boat
I really love him, I really do
I hope that he feels that too
I turn my attention to my friends
They give me support and sends
Me on a journey, it takes a while
But in the end, I start to smile
I can't forget my family, they're the best
But part of it is on a quest
To fight the frightful cancer
But we hope the answer
Is that he will survive
And that he will thrive
I do hope so, because if I lost him
It would be like losing a limb
And they're the most important things to me
So I wish bad luck would leave me be.

Natasha Mason (13)
Ripon College, Ripon

My Horse

I love it when Spirit gallops around the field like mad.
I love it when I ride him, he doesn't go backwards, but my last horse went forwards.
I love it when he says please, by bowing his head.
I love it when he is scared and he cuddles up to me.
I love it when he neighs for food.
I love it when he is eating his little face off.
I love him because Spirit is mine and he always will be forever.

Brionie Grout (13)
Ripon College, Ripon

Journey Of Life

Life is violence, fight it
Life is a promise, keep it
Life is a confession, prepare for it
Life is a dream, dream it
Life is frustration, face it
Life is a song, sing it
Life is an adventure, explore it
Life is a struggle, accept it
Life is precious, cherish it.

Life is a seed, plant it
Life is despair, spare it
Life is a journey, travel it
Life is beauty, admire it
Life is a challenge, commit to it
Life is sorrow, overcome it
Life is a game, play it
Life is fame, enjoy it
Life is music, listen to it
Life is me and forever will be.

Wongai Musemwa (13)
Ripon College, Ripon

School

I do not like school,
But some people think it's cool.

Break and lunch,
People just munch.

Lessons are rubbish,
I wish they were fun.

The good thing about it is,
I see my friends and people I like.

The school is a mess
And really doesn't impress.

In the winter,
It's always freezing.

The uniform is dull,
And no one likes it.

So basically Ripon College,
Only helps your knowledge.

Naomi Hodgson (13)
Ripon College, Ripon

My Dream

If I had a dream car that's what my life would be about
Driving fast and making the engine shout
Driving around, around, causing a stir
Then whizzing off as a blur
I want a car that shows money
A fast convertible in case the weather is sunny

Some people would laugh and take the mick
They might say the body is sick
Theyre jealous I got my dream
This is Philip Kent and I'm thirteen.

Philip Kent (13)
Ripon College, Ripon

The Storm

It was getting cloudier and louder,
It was smashing and clashing.

It was getting longer like the conga.
It was angry like Mr Facoltey.

It was like a mean man's face at the end of a race.
It was a red-back spider hating a can of cider.

It was Daniel's arm after he went on a farm
And mucked out the pigs with a bottle of figs.

It was sipping its wine until late, at nine.
It was like my mate's face in the morning, when it was calling
Like it was falling.

It was lightning like a fight happening
It was grinning like he just ate something minging.

It was a storm like a shouting horn.

Sarah Blanchard (14)
Ripon College, Ripon

When The Last Teardrop Falls

It's so hard to lose the one you love
To finally have to say goodbye
You try to be strong, but the pain keeps holding on,
And all that you can do is cry.
Deep within your heart, you know it's time to move on.
When the fairy tale
That you once knew has gone.

When the last teardrop falls,
I'll still be holding on to all of our memories
And all of what used to be.
If there was just one wish I could be granted here today
It would be to have you right back by my side.

Lydia Stevenson (13)
Ripon College, Ripon

My Hamster

I love it when I play with my hamster,
I like cleaning her out every Thursday,
I am her favourite owner out of me and my friend next door,
I give my hamster food and water every three days,
I sometimes get her out before me and my little sister go to bed,
She wakes up when Mum makes tea because she can smell the food,
I love it when she crawls on my shoulders,
My hamster sometimes nibbles me, but I don't mind,
I love it when I see my hamster climb into her cage,
I love my hamster.

Stephanie Numan (12)
Ripon College, Ripon

Vegas

Opportunity upon opportunity
Bigger upon better
Vegas is the place to be.

Brilliance upon magnificence
Casino upon Bellagio
Vegas is the place to see.

From five star to super cars
From billboards to casino doors
You'll never wish to leave.

From shopping malls to curtain calls
From Elvis wannabes to the real Jay-Z
It's better than make believe.

So . . .

Vegas is the real deal
Vegas is the ultimate place
Vegas is what you strive for
If legendary is the ace.

Derek Van Der Westhuizen (14)
Ripon Grammar School, Ripon

The Poem Of Anne Frank

We cannot make a sound, not up here.
In this place above the ground, everyone could hear!
Floorboards will creak
But we still cannot speak.
Crossing fingers the tap does not leak.
Tiniest sound, it just takes one more
To have us exposed to the outside war.
I have the soul of a teen, struggling inside
Forcing itself out, not wanting to hide!
Poor palest faces stained with tears
Could not hide deep, dark fears.

Letting out screams
These must be horrible dreams!
Opening our eyes,
Not being surprised
Still trapped up here
Sound of footsteps is a sound like 'Oh dear'
Fist on door.

As it falls to the floor
Fire of guns
Yet nowhere to run
I lay in the bath
Trying to laugh
Screams
Shouts
Fists
Gunshots
Hand around my leg
Pulling me away
From my diary
My parents
My annex
My life.

Pallas Stroer-Jarvis (11)
Ripon Grammar School, Ripon

Colours

Blue is the sky
Blue is two thirds of the world
Blue is the sea
Blue is cool
Blue is . . .

Red is anger
Red is blood
Red is the worst
Red is in all of us
Red is . . .

Yellow is the sun
Yellow is the glow of stars
Yellow is the light
Yellow is the warmest colour
Yellow is . . .

Green is the grass
Green is brilliant
Green is the best of all there is
Green is the leaves on the trees
Green is . . .

Black is dull
Black is the thing we hate the most
Black is death
Black is the worst
Black is . . .

Purple is alright, but not the best
Purple is in all shades, dark to light
Purple is the colour some like and some hate
Purple is weird
Purple is . . .

Thomas Louden (11)
Ripon Grammar School, Ripon

Flowers

Daffodils,
Their golden trumpets play a beautiful tune,
Their petals silky and soft,
Forming a pathway to Heaven,
Filling the air with calming scents,
Daffodils.

Roses,
A melody of sweet smells fill the air,
Folds upon folds of soft, satin petals,
Crimson red, red as a ruby, red as blood,
Brightening the fine, fresh gardens,
Roses.

Bluebells,
Crowded round the English forests,
Like gorgeous women chatting in the woods,
Thousands of them, having a tea party,
Swaying and dancing in the cool breeze,
Bluebells.

Hibiscus,
Made of all the colours of the sunset,
Giving Florida a tropical air,
Growing in the bright warm sun,
Bringing colour to sunny coasts,
Hibiscus.

Heather,
Spreading magenta on the British hills,
Blooming on the mossy banks,
Clashing with the green of the grass,
Adding colour to the landscape,
Heather.

Dana Julia Turner (11)
Ripon Grammar School, Ripon

Unknown

As night closes in and the sun kisses the world goodnight the moon comes out to rule over the land.

The beast awakens.

As the stars watch over the sleeping landscape catching every detail with their twinkling eyes and the trees, silhouetted against the moon's light, create an eerie atmosphere that is only right for this night.

The beast awakens.

As the shadows of long lost souls creep around searching hopelessly for what their hearts desire and the pitch-black of the night overwhelms the Earth and consumes every object in its path.

The beast awakens.

The beast awakens.

The beast awakens.

The beast, mighty and heroic, not scared of the spies that are always there, always watching you, disguised as stars until the moon's reign ends and the sun takes the throne. Not scared of the moon itself and the evil which it casts over the world, possessing every creature's mind. But not the majestic beast.

Unstoppable.

Even the moon and its evil presence retreat at the sight of the beast.

All is silent.

The beast.

The beast.

What is the beast?

Poppy Stanton (11)
Ripon Grammar School, Ripon

What I Think Of You

I love the way you hold my hand,
And catch me when I fall,
I love the way your smile melts my heart,
And breaks down my guarding walls.
I love the way your blue eyes twinkle,
When they're looking into mine,
I love the way you give me butterflies,
And they will never disappear in time.

I don't like how you think you're right,
Every single time I'm not,
I don't like how you get me anxious,
And make my stomach twist into a knot.
I don't like the way I forgive you,
Every single time,
And I don't like how you know you'll always
Have a place in this heart of mine.

I wish I could capture,
Those special moments we share,
I wish I could be with you,
Here, there and everywhere.
I wish that I could stay in your arms forever,
Because I feel so safe with you,
I wish that I could always be what you deserve,
And for you to know I will always stay true to you.

But what I love the most about you,
Is that you're my best friend.
And what I wish most definitely
Is that you're the one for me and for us to never end.

Sophie Charlton (13)
Ripon Grammar School, Ripon

Beach - Haikus

Day
Sun shines on the sea
Mighty blades slice through the sky
Bask in its glory.

Waves crash on the beach
As far as the eye can see
Glistening movement.

Countless grains of sand
Golden quilt covers the coast
Plain simplicity.

Elegant palm trees
Protection against the sun
Nature's umbrella.

Night
The light of the moon
Creates mental images
Spotlight in the sea.

Feel the cold sea waves
Splash around our frozen feet
Water's orchestra.

Supple sand unseen
The black shroud encases us
Eternal darkness.

Unseen obstacle
Sleeping in the water's edge
Beware of the tree.

Ranjeet Shahi (14)
Ripon Grammar School, Ripon

Accept It

It sweeps like a hurricane,
Wrecking carefully made plans,
Putting a gun in the face of order.

I was told that I'd be fine,
That life would resume,
Minus one.

And we can't accept it.

We learn to move on,
Even love again,
But it's never the same.

That moment of reflection,
Backwards is painful,
What ifs, they're deadly.

And we can't accept it.

The tears are less,
The pain's still there,
Pictures surround these walls.

The wake of the hurricane,
Has left pain and sorrow,
And a time for happiness.

We will accept it.

Soaked with memories,
Normality has resumed.

Jack Lale (15)
Ripon Grammar School, Ripon

Lucky Star

All the stars in the sky,
They sparkle and shine.
Of all of them up there,
One of them is mine.

They light up the world,
Under the deep purple sky.
My star's out there somewhere,
I'll find, I'll try.

Although outsized by far,
By the glowing, white moon,
My star still matters,
And I'll find it soon.

Even though there are billions,
And trillions of stars,
We all reach for the one,
That we can call ours.

And I am wishing,
That I'll sit still,
And that thousands of miles,
Will seem like the M1.

For although you are thousands,
Of light years away,
I know I will find you,
My one lucky star.

Ashleigh Messenger (13)
Ripon Grammar School, Ripon

Culinary Perfection

It covered me in gunk,
It smothered me in slime,
It rumbled at my mother,
These were not good times . . .

I tried to stop it happening,
I tried to shut it up,
It just continued angrily . . .
Getting rather rough.

I almost couldn't bear it,
I ran to find defence,
Couldn't find anyone actually,
Now it's creepy and tense.

The police were away on business,
Ambulance had 'other job's' too,
I did try ringing the fire brigade,
Reply, 'What's wrong with you?'

I began to panic at this point,
My heart of dread and frost,
The beast was going to kill me,
All hope was lost . . .

Just as I thought it was over,
My sis ran in and coughed,
Reaching for the plug socket,
She switched the blender off.

Billy Holdsworth (15)
Ripon Grammar School, Ripon

Untitled

I could write this poem
About my love . . .
His smile, eyes, floppy hair . . .
But instead I think I shall write
About the ones who are always there.

The one with the incredible strength,
Of character and mind,
I wish I could be more like her -
She taught me courage.
For others' opinions she does not care.

The one with whom
Every moment is precious.
Pearly laughter, sparkling eyes;
Moments are never empty.
I know she'll be there all the time.

And the one in whose company
I can always escape.
With him I can just be;
Stop thinking, never afraid to cry.

So next time you're writing a poem
Of sticky, inky angst;
How love is never fair,
Pause; take a look in the heart
And I think of the ones who will always be there.

Eleanor Duffield (17)
Ripon Grammar School, Ripon

Snow - Haiku

The gloom of whiteness,
The deep silence of the snow,
Obscures what we know.

Megan Aspinall (17)
Ripon Grammar School, Ripon

You Can't Do That

One thing that everyone has is . . .
Singing lessons
Please Mum can I do that?
No Timmy, you are far too croaky for that
Then if I can't do that what can I do . . .
Swimming?
Maybe next year Timmy, you're too young now.
Can we go to . . .
Soft play today?
No Timmy, you're too old for that.
I know a good one, can I do . . .
Climbing Mum?
No Timmy, you know you're scared of heights.
Then could I possibly do . . .
Shopping in town with friends?
No Tlimmy, it's too much money!
Perhaps I could do . . .
Nothing?
No Timmy, (to think that, you could be bored)
If you're really that bored you could do . . .
Homework
House chores
Or you could look after the dog we bought you last year,
Because you claimed you had nothing to do then, as well.

Emily Watson (11)
Ripon Grammar School, Ripon

Winter Tree - Haiku

The old tree stands still
Humiliated, naked
Winter has fallen.

Thomas Lonsdale (12)
Ripon Grammar School, Ripon

Nom

Nom is a thing, a meaning, a purpose
Nom is a flame, deep within all of us
Nom is to you
Nom is to me
Nom is a feeling
Nom is free

Nom is a puzzle, a mind game, a chase
Nom is forever, no, never a race
Nom is a beast it snarls in the moonlight
Catch it with a net, it'll put up a fight
Nom is a dance, a feeling of glee
Nom lives deep within you and me
Nom is a chain, links never broken
Nom is silent, words never spoken.

Nom is to life
Nom is to death
Nom is a drug, like crystal meth
Nom makes us high
Happy with power
Nom makes our life one big happy hour
Nom is a thing
Nom is forever
Nom is a saying, never say never.

Reece Farren (15)
Ripon Grammar School, Ripon

Tsunami - Haiku

Crash! My world destroyed
The huge wave; a great surprise
Did I deserve this?

Sophie Glover (15)
Ripon Grammar School, Ripon

Counter Clockwork

Hands move in one direction
Hours move in the other
I am one of the new generation
But still you are stuck with the former
I will move onwards; can't wind my way up
Help, she says; frozen within

I have a plan
Like a blazing fire
I will rise
I will dance, I will be

You will fall
A sodden, smoking mass
Collapsed under the timbers
You failed to build . . .

Streaming like a leopard on the wind . . .
A gunshot rattles through the air
Like the steady tick of the clock
Sticking without care
Forwards
Unmoving
Waiting
To rewind.

Jessica Burgess (17)
Ripon Grammar School, Ripon

Our Love Tree

Blossom from a cherry tree
Frivolous, it dances merrily.
Crystal drops began to tease
The branches swaying in the breeze.

That day it grew
We both knew
This was the start of something new.

It grew and grew so highly
As far as the eye could see
Roots penetrating the virgin soiled
It spread, twisted and coiled.

The veins stretched strong
Stretching to the throng
Of our mystical song.

As it reached its peak
It began to look bleak.
It rotted from within
Due to multiple sin.

As they say
As a gravestone it lay
There every single day.

Zoe Harrison (17)
Ripon Grammar School, Ripon

Today - Haiku

A long time ago
Slaves were bought and sold, cattle
They still are today.

Jonathan J Bucktrout (15)
Ripon Grammar School, Ripon

The Match

We walk to the turf,
Stomachs churning,
Legs burning,
Brains whirring,
Studs grate on the green surface, stains of brown soil emerge,
Like blood to a cut.
Your hand reaches longingly to the ground below,
Numb against the wisps of grass.
The whistle pierces the air, light scatters and fragments through expedient clouds.
Watching, waiting, willing.
An eager foot rolls the ball off the centre circle.
The mind goes blank.
Impulse takes over.
Control,
Pass,
Cross,
Dribble,
Tackle,
Shoot.
The body pulls itself round the pitch, grinding, climbing.
The mind is helpless. Thoughts useless.

Lawrence Holmes (16)
Ripon Grammar School, Ripon

Shadows

A dark silhouette watching you when you sleep,
Feeding off your soul,
Forever growing stronger;
The murderous stranger in your nightmares,
The one that everyone fears the most
Can you see the shadow?
He's standing right behind you.

Sophie Ryan (12)
Ripon Grammar School, Ripon

Polo My Favourite Pony

I know where you are,
I know where you went,
But my darling, it wasn't me who sent
You to your new home,
Polo you see,
If it was my decision,
You'd still be with me.

I remember when it seemed to me,
You'd be with me for eternity,
I guess I was wrong,
Polo you see,
Even though you're gone,
Now I miss you dearly,
You mean the world to me.

We rode for very long,
And I always sang a song,
When I was on your back,
We always had a laugh,
Polo you see,
And I really, really hope,
I hope you miss me.

Lucy Chapman (13)
Ripon Grammar School, Ripon

My Best Friend

I owe you my heart, because you've always been there,
And I'd do anything, to let you know I care.

I owe you my strength, because you've lifted me up,
And you were there for me, even when I messed up.

I'm uncertain of a lot of things, but I know this much is true,
I consider you my best friend, and I'd die for you.

Katie Utley (14)
Ripon Grammar School, Ripon

Forgotten Memories

Memories linger between its threads
Feeling lost and forgotten
Folded away in the dark drawer
It still hears the cries of children
Crying for their mothers.

It used to be as soft as clouds
But now old and chewed
Is looking frayed and dirty
In a comforting way.

To previous owners
It was their childhood
To some it's an old woolly
Scruffy blanket.

If it could it would cry
Cry tears of neglect and pain
The piercing pain
For the one it loved
And loved the most
Someone who loved the sad bundle
As much as it loved her.

Beth Grimmer (12)
Ripon Grammar School, Ripon

Reach New Heights

We're singing, for freedom
I'm ready for, still waiting for
I'm thinking that maybe, just maybe
Tell me what you're gonna do
We'll be the elements
We'll be the sky
We'll reach new heights
Ready, set, fly.

Tom Gott (15)
Ripon Grammar School, Ripon

A Memory Of The Past

A memory of the past,
A chequered pattern holds the memory,
Strapped tight by a button,
The isolated handwriting,
Stuck within a pattern of fences,
Candlelight is a blessing,
Lost within souls,
Fragile, frail and *trapped.*

A memory of the past,
The secrets it holds are yet to be told,
Screams yell from within it,
Insecurity mutters constantly,

All alone, hidden,
It hears something a brief whisper,
A thought is told inside,
Unaware, saddened and gone.

They're here . . .

No more.

A memory of the past and of horror.

Will Stobbs (11)
Ripon Grammar School, Ripon

Remember

A flash lights up the blanket of darkness,
Illuminating the night sky.
It feels like there's an audience,
Peeking through the holes in the floor of Heaven.
I stand there, watching.
I stand there, remembering.
I stand there, waiting,
Until everything comes back.

Amy Hughes (16)
Ripon Grammar School, Ripon

Father And Son

Tired stone crumbles to the ground, green creepers
Snake up walls of the abandoned and ruined castle.

A brave old knight, in shining armour, carrying a battle-hardened sword,
Gallops over the well worn ground,
Readying himself for where he must go.

A brilliant sunrise floods over the land, he doesn't see
The flocks of birds flying south for the oncoming winter.
Over the hills a battle awaits. Is he too late?

As darkness sweeps over the path, the courageous
Knight pushes ahead, praying he won't be devoured by
The hand of the daunting devil.

Dust covers the exhausted ground, a gateway to Hell
Opening its doors, ready to welcome the souls of the
Already dead.

It's over, despair, the sight he sees as he across the
Ridge to his final destination. They are everywhere,
Scattered all over the ground, bodies, corpses of the
Departed, they sent chills through his body, as he scans
Them looking for the one he loves, one particular person.

Lucy Wicks (11)
Ripon Grammar School, Ripon

Subservient Incontinence

'Don't talk to the dog,'
Said the voice from the kitchen.
'Don't touch the dog,'
Said the voice from the kitchen,
The dog is peeing,
The mop is coming.
. . . The voice is not amused;
Disinfectant has to be used.

Angus Johnston (15)
Ripon Grammar School, Ripon

Macbeth!

There goes the bell, one, two, three,
The murderous bell so this must be.
I make my way up to the castle walls,
And hear the witches' babbling calls.
Treading on pebbles all the way,
Hoping they don't let my plan out where they lay.
There hoots the barn owl and I'm standing at the stair,
A bloodstained dagger appears in mid air.
The sleeping guards lay quiet and still,
By the hand of my lady's will.
Was this fate or was this a dream?
But I must go a long with this evil scheme.
For I must not let my beautiful wife down,
As I make my way in I see my soon to be crown.
There lays King Duncan in his gold-covered bed,
Raising the dagger one tear that I shed.
Falls down my cheek as the dagger plunges into his heart,
For Lady Macbeth thought this plan was so smart.
I walked back swiftly, quietly and quick,
Feeling so guilty and physically sick.
I fear this will haunt me for life.

Caitlin Ramsey (11)
Ripon Grammar School, Ripon

Dogs - Haikus

Dogs are sweet and soft
They are filled with love and care
No one can doubt them

Dogs are always cool
Dogs can tell you something's wrong
Dogs will never fade.

David Ramsden (11)
Ripon Grammar School, Ripon

Tornado

Mother of nature most dangerous being
Vortex of the wind and the trees
Buildings, water, cars and people I see in my street
In the air they scream for help
They're carried away in this thing
This thing is deadly - I want to go outside.
But my mum and dad refuse
I see my friend screaming for help
I don't care what they say
I want to go outside now
To help him
Saving him now - not tomorrow
I go outside
I am swept off my feet
I scream for help
I am swept
Away
Away
and
Away.

David Prestwich (11)
Ripon Grammar School, Ripon

Night Walk

The tall dark shadows danced in the moonlight,
The sound of breaking twigs echoed off the trees.
Trees stood tall like a never-ending skyscraper,
Stars like yellow eyes gazing down at you.

The gentle sound of running water glided through the air,
Water reflecting a sparkling pool of stars.
The moonlight beamed down from above,
The hoot of an owl pierced the night's air.

Henry Worrall (14)
Ripon Grammar School, Ripon

Horses

Riding, racing, rolling
On a warm day
Grooming, washing, picking, feeding
On a winter night.
Up and down the field
On a frosty morning
Walking, trotting, cantering
On a Saturday afternoon
Brushing, stroking
On a Sunday night
Jumping big and small
Practising for the show
Rugs, boots, manes, and tails
Going on the trailer ramp
Waiting, wishing, warming up
Going round the ring
Riding, washing, trotting,
Galloping, jumping
Boots and trailer ramps
I'm ready, go, go.

Lauren Pybus (11)
Ripon Grammar School, Ripon

Ode To Lucinda

Her hair is as yellow as my planner,
Her eyes are as blue as Finlay's refill pad.
Her nose is carved by angels.

Her teeth are as straight as the biro I write with,
She is as beautiful as Hermione,
And I am proud to call her my friend.

Kate Robinson (16)
Ripon Grammar School, Ripon

The Horse Of Thunder

He stood on the hill
Framed by the light
The horse of thunder
Paused in flight.
His midnight coat was a smooth, sleek gloss
As dark and as black as the night
While the blaze that ran down his face
Was a bright crystal white
No one could contain him
Or break his awful might
Yet before me the horse of thunder stood
Framed by the pale light
He tossed his mighty head
His mane flowing in the breeze
His shrill piercing whinny
Echoed off the trees
He reared up high above me
Eyes full of an angry light
Then he turned and sped away
The horse of thunder as one with the night.

Juliet Fenlon (13)
Ripon Grammar School, Ripon

Fire

Fire, burning, hot
Glowing, bright embers,
Sun-like, the fire provides light and warmth.

Above the fire falls rain,
And in seconds,
Darkness.

Adam Haswell (15)
Ripon Grammar School, Ripon

Silence, Please . . .

All I can hear is the scribbling of pencils,
The clock strikes two in the background,
Five minutes left says the teacher,
I look over to my right,
All I see are hundreds of people writing their final answers,
But I've already finished, I've already finished my final exam.

Check, check and check again says the voice in my head,
Fill in all those empty spaces,
I look up at the clock, ten seconds left,
Tick, tock, tick, tock,
'Put your pens down,' shouts the teacher at the front.
We all turn round, look at one another,
Mouthing to each other, how did you find it?
But we all know if we get caught our grades could be gone, just like that,

We all walk out, row after row,
Until, finally it's my turn to go,
Goodbye papers, goodbye pens and finally goodbye silence,
please . . .

Jessica Bryden (13)
Ripon Grammar School, Ripon

Night Owl

The hunter, the hunted
The night owl watches its prey
Its eyes fresh and glowing amber
Alone and still
The night owl remains frozen
A movement below
Wings outstretched
The night owl swoops
Silence
The hunter, the hunted.

Toby Kinread (15)
Ripon Grammar School, Ripon

Mysterious

Have you ever seen a shape?
Moving through the night?
Ever thought what it might be?
A shadow, a figure, a light?

But what the mystery is,
Is where this shape may be going?
To your house, your school or a nearby park.
Maybe on a forever going journey.

Could it be real?
Or a confusing nightmare?
Is it the future?
Or an ordinary sight?
Could it be you?
Or a lonesome mystery?

No one will know.
Possibly ever!

Sophie Spick (12)
Ripon Grammar School, Ripon

Regret

A burning feeling in your body
It's coursing through your veins,
An anger slowly bubbles up,
A stinging kind of rage.
Pounding in your brain one minute,
A stabbing pain the next,
It steals the breath within your lips
It wraps around your neck,
Scaly talons pull you down,
You know you won't forget,
And all alone within the dark,
Are you and your regret.

Claudia Seeger (14)
Ripon Grammar School, Ripon

Still In Love

I've just lost a massive part of me
I have a broken heart in me
There's a girl I thought I could work with,
But it turns out she wasn't worth it,

The annoying thing is I still love her,
Even if she loves another,
I want to be with her forever,
Though we'll never be together.

I had my shot with love,
But I guess it wasn't enough
I want to make it work,
I want it so badly it hurts.

If only she gave me a chance,
Maybe then we'd have romance,
I'll have to let her go,
But I'm still in love though.

Chandler Brewer (14)
Ripon Grammar School, Ripon

Where Would You Go If You Could Go Back In Time?

Would you go back to the world's creation
Or to the Queen's Coronation.
Would you go see Elvis die on the loo
Or see World War II?
Would you go back and see the Great Fire of London
Or see someone in the dungeon?
Would you see Apollo 13 land on the moon
Or see Ghandi using a loom?
Would you go see Princess Diana's car crash
Or Hitler with his moustache?
Would you go back to the start of the war in Iraq
Or would you plain and simple not go back?

Annabelle Ayliffe (13)
Ripon Grammar School, Ripon

The Journey Of Time

Day to night, light to dark
Sunrise to sunset, rest to work
Morning to afternoon, work to play
This is the never-ending journey of time.

Past to present, present to future
Yesterday to today, today to tomorrow
Tradition to now, now to modernisation
This is the never-ending journey of time.

Dinosaurs to extinction, extinction to new life
Cavemen to humans, humans to aliens
Belief to religion, religion to gods
This is the never-ending journey of time.

The weather cycle
The life cycle
The never-ending cycle of life
The journey of time will never end.

Simon Evans (15)
Ripon Grammar School, Ripon

Orange

Firing emotion
Hot and fiery,
Smells like jungle air
Blowing in the sunset;
Raging winds
Helping it grow,
As fire spreads
There may be death,
But always new life,
With a good
Outcome.
Orange.

Patrick John Moon (11)
Ripon Grammar School, Ripon

Equilibrium

A never-ending world of thoughts,
Where happiness and hatred collide,
Where regret and hope comes knocking,
The dark void of imagination.

Love, excitement, happiness,
Themes which often occur,
Regret, sadness, grief,
Burdens which tend to linger.

All feature a point of existence,
Yet sometimes hard to understand,
Why put up with stress, anger?
Why can't elation be constant?

Without pain, woe, sorrow,
Opposites wouldn't have a place,
Optimism, merriment would cease to exist,
Ever changing thoughts would not persist.

Sally Pitts (14)
Ripon Grammar School, Ripon

Midnight For A Student

The darkest hours aren't always at night.
But my heart sinks a fathom
As I take in sight,
Of it.
It lies on my desk, unmoving,
My head starts to throb, dull, blunt.
The silence of the night is far from soothing,
I stare balefully through the clock,
The luminous numbers searing my heavy-lidded eyes.
Again it would seem,
I've left it too late,
I pick up the pen, sleep can wait.

Ashley Lowe (17)
Ripon Grammar School, Ripon

Four Seasons

The leaves fall,
Down, down to the floor,
Trees appear small,
All across the moors.

Cold harsh winters,
Snow all around,
Long cold winters,
Frost on the ground.

Beautiful spring,
Daffodils grow,
Birds they do sing,
Farmers do sow.

Long hot summers,
Rain again and again,
Bright blue sky,
That summers do send.

Andrew Harrison (16)
Ripon Grammar School, Ripon

Friends Are

Friends are the sun to its ray,
Friends are the daisy in a sunflower field.
Friends are the light in a dark tunnel,
Friends are the only star in the sky,
Friends are the cloud on a clear blue day,
Friends are the butterfly in a swarm of caterpillars,
Friends are the SpongeBob to his Patrick,
Friends are the people who look at you for who you are,
Friends are black,
Friends are white,
Friends are true,
Friends stand by you.

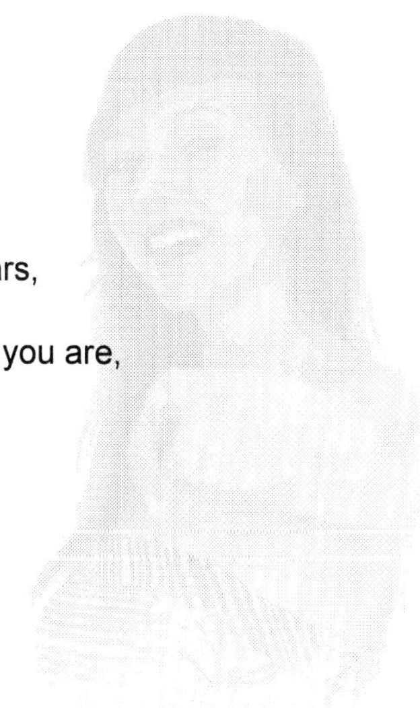

Evangeline Don (13)
Ripon Grammar School, Ripon

The Vest

Running; feet pounding the earth,
Moving; round and round the track,
An athlete; running for Britain,
The vest, wafting in the breeze.

The vest; a British vest,
The vest; a brilliant white vest,
The vest; a red streaked vest,
The vest; an athlete's vest.

The vest; holding memories,
The vest; feeling proud yet sad,
The vest; thinking of its winnings,
The vest; remembering what is lost.

The vest; remembering the good,
The vest; always winning its race,
The vest; will always be there,
The vest; of my dad.

Ben Pease (12)
Ripon Grammar School, Ripon

The Way

I love the way you look at me
Like I'm the only one you can see
I love the way you hold me
Like there's nowhere you'd rather be
I love the way you kiss me
Like each time is the first
I love the way you compliment
Even when I look my worst
I love the way you protect me
So there's nothing I should fear at all
I love the way you love me
So a tear will never fall.

Demi Farrar (15)
Ripon Grammar School, Ripon

The Horizon

As the morning light splashed over the fields
My bare feet soaked up fresh dew
And my hands skimmed each tree that I passed
Each one rougher than the other.

I leant against one of these trees
Gazing out as the sun was reborn
A dragonfly flicked from pond to pond
Wings like glittering diamonds.

I walked on for what felt like forever
Lilac heather was dotted around as far as the eye can see
An elegant swan rippled the water of a shimmering lake
And a kingfisher flew overhead.

And even though I knew
My journey would never end
What a beautiful thing to encounter
To try to find the horizon.

Georgia Stuart-Mills (12)
Ripon Grammar School, Ripon

Grief

Engulfed by the depth of this pit,
Tears flood my defences, I mouth something inadequate, lost.

Gripped motionless as a multitude of bubbles rise,
I am paralysed, ripped up.

Time balances then tips and I drown,
My chest tears, butchered.

Flailing limbs reaching upwards for before -
I find only a still warm expanse. Strangled moans.

This sad pool of separation settles,
I am brought up, lifeless.

Hebe Beardsall (17)
Ripon Grammar School, Ripon

Confused

As I sat there all tense, with my knees close to my beating
heart . . .

I listened . . .
A tall shadow stood. Big and bold on my doorstep . . .
With my head firmly clasped between my knees . . .
I waited . . .

The figure on my doorstep raised one hand. Then pulled out of its pocket an
elastic band . . .
What it did next was different, I know . . .
It took the elastic band and made it snow!

By now I was confused.

I stood up and walked towards the door . . .
Then suddenly my vision became poor . . .
The man on my doorstep was suddenly . . .

Gone . . .

Katie Moorhouse (12)
Ripon Grammar School, Ripon

Darkness

The looming, all consuming darkness destroys its victims' souls.
It grabs and squeezes, pulls and sucks.
Then it twirls and drains out all the guts.
It breaks free at night and is captured at morning.
Its eyes are like moons and its teeth are like spikes.

Drifting down the hallway, slipping under doors.
It watches people in their beds, waiting with its claws.
It tends to go for children, as they're a fresher meal.
Getting ready for a meal, it spots a speck of light.
It drags its luminous body under the foot of a bed.
Now the sun has risen, it waits for the living dead . . .

Benjamin Wayne (11)
Ripon Grammar School, Ripon

An Autumn Scene

Crunchy leaves by my feet,
A golden carpet on the street.

Leaves falling fast,
Summer's in the past.

A fire roaring, people snoring.
Lovely colours brighten the morning.

A coolness starts to fill the air.
Halloween, a fright, a scare!

Birds were tweeting, now they're fleeting.

Warm hot food, a cosy mood.

Another birthday comes and goes,
Shivering winds and chilly toes.

The leaves once all dark and green
But here at last an autumn scene.

Daniel Robert Cushnie (14)
Ripon Grammar School, Ripon

Hats

They come and go, old and new.
On rainy days, snowy days and hot days.
We adventure the blizzards and storms
On your head, do hats!
On sweaty heads, hairy heads, baldies too.
We sit and watch many things.
People love us and hate us.
For long and short terms we sit and wait.
Fluffy, bobble, baseball too!
We ski, ride and swim.
We go everywhere

Do hats!

George Pearson (11)
Ripon Grammar School, Ripon

Food

Food is evolving from day to day
Bread to croissants, apples to pears
Mars to Milky Way, water to juice.

Food never stops, we want more and more
We have food groups, food fights
Fast food, food competitions.

Food makes you famous, food makes you rich
Food makes you taller, food makes you sleepy
Food makes you hungry, food makes you.

We have the biggest food, the tastiest food
The most expensive food, the average food
Food statistics, food programmes, food fanatics.

It has to be said;
We humans are a miraculous and marvellous race,
And we love food.

James Sharkey (14)
Ripon Grammar School, Ripon

Peer Pressure

P ushing me to do things,
E veryone egging me on.
E ven if I don't want to do it,
R eason is gone in a group.

P retending I like things I don't,
R espect is what I crave,
E veryone is the same,
S ucking up, for a name.
S ense goes out the window,
U surping to get to the top.
R oles reversed, you do the same,
E ven though, you know it's lame.

James Woolfenden (15)
Ripon Grammar School, Ripon

Microscopic

In the water since bones roamed the ground,
My mouth frozen with words that were forgotten.
One microscopic memory that hangs in the back of my mind like an old,
Tattered sheet.

Nerves Exist

One encouragement
Sounds the start,
The others follow. Hearts excited, it begins.
Everything is waiting.

I go up, mind whirring
Introduction becomes a flash of polysyndetic patterning.
Like a deer, caught in the headlights, no way back . . .

Caught, and stuck in a spotlight of shame.
Shadows cover my eyes, no noise . . .
No more curtain call dreams.

Billie Tweddle (11)
Ripon Grammar School, Ripon

The Old Warrior

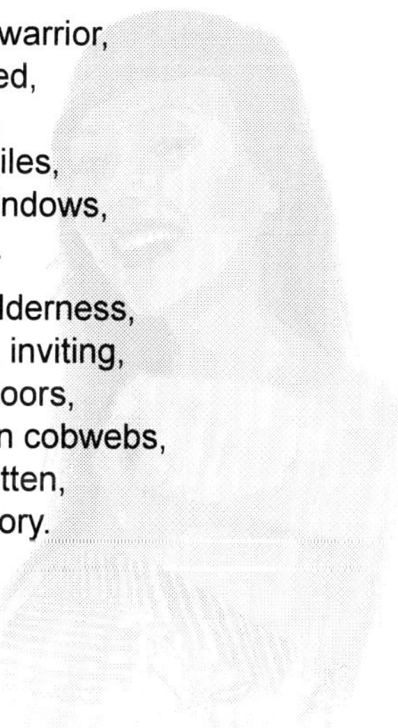

Standing like an old, forgotten warrior,
Lost in time, tired and dated,
Covered in battle scars,
Broken chimneys, missing tiles,
Flapping shutters, shattered windows,
A real seasoned soldier.

Sinking, disappearing into the wilderness,
An open, battered door, waiting, inviting,
Creaking floors, squeaking doors,
Old, weathered trophies, covered in cobwebs,
Deserted, abandoned, forgotten,
Just an old discarded memory.

Sam Close (13)
Ripon Grammar School, Ripon

Parents

P arents pick you up when you're feeling down.
They're A mazing in every way.
They're R eliable and someone who you can trust.
Your E ntertainment costs them a lot of money.
Everlasti N g love is what they give.
T hey care for you no matter what.
They S pend thousands of pounds on their children.

P eople often ignore what their parents have done for them.
A gain and again we never listen to them.
R epeating our mistakes time and time again.
E very time we annoyed them, they forgave us.
N eeding our parents' love more and more as we get older.
T rustworthy and kind most of the time.
Keeping us S afe and healthy was one of their main priorities.

Matthew Binks (13)
Ripon Grammar School, Ripon

The Fisherman

The fisherman sits under a handful of stars;
A sea of a sparkling, splattering mess;
No one can tell what he is feeling;
For he is emotionless.

The villagers ask where he lives;
But he just laughs and carries on;
His laugh is like a trickling stream;
His smile like the sun.

He almost never catches anything;
But when he does he lets it go;
It's like Mother Nature made him herself,
The immortal fisherman.

Joy Sutcliffe (11)
Ripon Grammar School, Ripon

The Cat

The cat.
She casts dark shadows down dimly lit roads;
Her eyes glisten like sapphires in the moonlight.
Midnight walker, dangerous and daring;
Prowler, stalker, beautiful and caring.

The cat.
She sneaks around at the dead of the night,
As black as her heart she wanders in darkness.
Sparkling eyes, no soul, no heart.
She's lonely and cries, but she's cold and dark.

The cat.
Lonely and broken she crawls through the night,
While her shadows dance in the glow of the stars.
Mischief maker, her life's a mystery.
Star gazer, now her life's history.

Laura Mackenzie (11)
Ripon Grammar School, Ripon

The Flower

I touch the flower,
A drop of water falls
And ricochets off the tiny
Yet vivid green leaf.
Within the army of identical green leaves
The ricocheted drop picks its next victim.
But before he can, the heavens open and
Gracefully welcome the great ball of fire
That is the sun.
He shows off his magnificent rays
Which, slowly but surely,
Soak up the dew drops.
The magic has gone.

Hannah Hale (15)
Ripon Grammar School, Ripon

The New Arrival

Something has happened,
Something has changed.
Whatever it is, things aren't
Quite the same.
When I got to my place in
My favourite chair,
Something or someone was already there.

It wasn't a cat or a bat or a frog,
In fact it was worse: because it was a dog.
Didn't they love me?
Was I a bad cat?
Because now he's moved in, all furry and fat.

Things could be better
Things could be OK
If only that dog would just go away.

Katie Veitch (11)
Ripon Grammar School, Ripon

What Does It Matter?

We work, work, with no say
What does it matter? We have no lips.
Man and bone shoulder out light.
What does it matter? We have no eyes.
Screeching, grinding cools the spine.
What does it matter? We have no ears.

A strand of light creeps,
We are revived:
Our ears open,
Our eyes open, and our lips open.

It is only then we realise
Sky is not the limit.

Christian Porter (15)
Ripon Grammar School, Ripon

The World

The world is life
The world is death
The world is happiness
The world is misery

The world

The world is food
The world is hunger
The world is love
The world is hate

The world

The world is battle
The world is forgiveness
The world is your world
But my world is mine.

Robert Wilmore (12)
Ripon Grammar School, Ripon

The Pyramids Rock!

Towering above the tallest skyscrapers,
Even taller than my dad,
Invented by the awesome Egyptians,
A lot of solid stone to make them,
So much stone with a ton of weight,
The pyramids rock!

Every day there's lots of building,
As well as lots of slaves,
Up at dawn and work till night,
Heave ho, heave ho,
At the end of the day they shout . . .
'The pyramids rock!'

Matthew Smith (11)
Ripon Grammar School, Ripon

War Is . . .

Wars are the terrifying battles of death,
The times of the century everyone dreads.
The pounding machine guns, the daring grenades,
The worrying panics, the endless first aid.

War is . . .

War is the anger and times you're away,
In the very Far East like Iraq or Bombay.
Wars are the terrorists, wars are the guns,
War is frantic, war isn't fun.

War is . . .

War should be banished, it just has to go.
Replace it with peace and let happy times show.
I could try to stop it, I could try if I want,
But all that I try, war will still go on.

Sam Noble (11)
Ripon Grammar School, Ripon

RIP

The old cemetery nothing but graves,
Darkness covers all,
Unrested souls lurk around,
All died from a broken heart,
Forgotten bodies lie there alone,
Their graves covered in dead roses,
Old pendants scratched and broken,
Filled with pictures of recent lovers,
If you ever see their spirits,
You can hear them say,
Ever felt invisible?

Francesca Law (11)
Ripon Grammar School, Ripon

The Dragonfly

My name is Andromeda, the beautiful dragonfly,
Left, right, left, right, flying through the sky,
Up and down at crazy heights searching for my prey,
Ooo, a helpless insect, he will have to pay.

A back of many colours, beautiful buzzing wings,
But when I see an insect, then it's zing, zing, zing!
Flying round a pond, in beautiful countryside,
Oh no, an angry bird! Now it's time to hide.

The bird has flown past now, at least I'm still alive,
It's far too hot today, I think I'll take a dive,
The sun is setting now, and everything is dark,
But I will hunt the night, a flying evil shark.

It's time to say goodbye, I am afraid to say,
But at least I can say, it's been a lovely day.

Max Crompton (13)
Ripon Grammar School, Ripon

The Storm

My eyes creaked open,
Like the door to my soul,
The burning light scalded me,
The crash and roar of the waves as they bit at my feet,
I felt the soft bed of sand underneath,
Cushioning me from the horror of my past . . .

It then came flooding back,
The dark treacherous storm bursting into the ship,
Sweeping away friend or foe
Into the black hollow monster that swallowed me whole.

Then the darkness came,
And the screams faded,
And the eyes closed.

Jemma Forster (15)
Ripon Grammar School, Ripon

Run-Away

I blow and make a wish,
Then watch them disappear into the sunset.
I lie in the sand watching the clouds,
Changing from pink to purple to black.
I feel the temperature drop,
Thinking how worried they must be.
I picture my mother crying by the fireplace,
And I cry with her.
I wait a little longer until I start to venture home,
I cross the street, and half cross the other,
Screech,
Crash,
Hit,
Black-out,
Death.

Elise Whincup (11)
Ripon Grammar School, Ripon

My Memory Book

It has people within its pages,
It shows different generations,
One family in one book,
Before it's been expanded.

If you saw it you'd think it was just a book,
If you looked inside,
You'd realise it's more special than that,
It's a book that holds memories.

It feels light and smooth,
You could keep it with you all day and all night,

Its colours are muddy brown and sunny orange and red,
Its pages are stained with tea,
And there's a black and white picture of *me*.

Lydia Bakes (12)
Ripon Grammar School, Ripon

The Hockey Game

The whistle is blown.
The push back is taken.
Tackles are made.
Stick on ball.
Up the wing.
Across the 'D'
Shot on target.
I make a save.
Kick the ball to the wing.
Pass follows pass.
We keep possession.
Into the 'D'.
A great shot.
Goal!
Back to the centre to start again.

Charlotte Clayton (13)
Ripon Grammar School, Ripon

Just Another Day

Early morning daylight engulfs my room,
Can it really be the morning so soon?
A minute ago I was lying in bed under a watery moon,
Why does the morning have to come so soon?

The comfort of my warm bed is begging me to stay,
The sudden clanging of my alarm reinforces another day,
The noise from a distant radio infiltrates my room,
Why does the morning have to come so soon?

Up, shower, dress, breakfast,
The day has really begun at last,
Money, keys, books in bag,
I wave goodbye.

Why does the morning have to come so soon?

Phoebe Lindsay (16)
Ripon Grammar School, Ripon

There's A Sound On The Horizon

There's a sound on the horizon,
It's getting closer and closer.
The sound of thundering hooves,
The sound of gloom and doom.
The thoughts in my head,
Wondering what to do,
To run or to hide?
Or to stand there with pride?
Or perhaps I could ride . . .?
That's it, I'll ride.
I'll ride the horses, make them stride
Through the Savannahs
Through the golden sand,
And through to the faraway
Promised land.

Rachael Pond (11)
Ripon Grammar School, Ripon

New Job

You have passed the test,
You're better than the rest.
The first challenge has come to an end,
But there are more around the bend.
There are new things to learn,
At first you'll want to return
To your old job, but you must endure
The hardships that'll happen for sure.
Because you'll soon know
That you'll have to undergo,
These tasks again and again and again.

Sam Easton (15)
Ripon Grammar School, Ripon

Creation

Yesterday I found out the reason
Why we're here today;
It all started when God sat down
And began to say;
'I will take on a challenge, that will continue for 7 days,
I will create the sun
And give it huge powerful rays.
I will create a magical liquid and nickname it H_20.
I will also invent a current
To keep all the water in flow.
But the most important thing that I will create,
Is something wonderful and impressively great,
It is you that's the most important, talented, cool and clever;
But when you start your creation journey,
Just remember never say never.'

Maxwell Morrison (11)
Ripon Grammar School, Ripon

The Great British Spud

The glorious
Sensation entering my
Mouth as I slowly lift the soft buttery
Potato into my open jaws, hoping for the
Next bite to come quicker. The mouth-watering
Wonder of all the spuds; The one that wears the
Jacket also holds my number one potato food
Badge, my taste buds are so lucky to have
It all the time, while the glorious
Sensation will always
Be mine!

Georgia Milligan (12)
Ripon Grammar School, Ripon

Love

My heart is gone
Left adrift in this heartless world
Flowing with my tears of sorrow
My soul is shattered
By the hammer of love

But my heart is on fire
With my love of this woman
The goddess of beauty
The goddess I love

Nothing will stop me
Following my heart
On its journey
For the one I desire
For the one I love.

Jamie Bowker (13)
Ripon Grammar School, Ripon

Memories

Memories last forever,
Memories fade.
Some wish to be forgotten,
No matter how they were made.

Memories last forever,
Memories fade.
The best ones will stay,
With you each day.

Memories last forever,
Memories fade . . .

Lucy Gittings (15)
Ripon Grammar School, Ripon

Cricket

The batsman gazing down the wicket,
Trembling with terror;
The bowler grasping the ball on its seam,
Staring at the batsman with pleasure.
Determined not to back away,
Picks up the bat,
And swings the heavy blade.

The ball rockets through the surface,
And hits him in the ribs,
He falls to the floor.
And pleads to be taken off the pitch,
The spectators on the edge of their seats,
Staring down at the wicket,
What a great day to be watching cricket.

Cameron O'Donnell (12)
Ripon Grammar School, Ripon

Without You

Without you, I'd be back to basics,
Without you, we would go into a black hole,
Without you, people would worship stone gods,
Without you, big words wouldn't be big anymore,
Without you, we would become cavemen,
Without you, I would die to join you,
Without you, clowns would perform to an empty audience,
Without you, there'd be no sun, no moon, no Mars, no life,
No city, no friends, no feelings, no happy days,
Without you . . .

Imogen Morgan (11)
Ripon Grammar School, Ripon

Once

(Inspired by 'The Boy In The Striped Pyjamas' by John Boyne)

Once there was a house, a shelter for me
Once there was transport to get me from place to place
Once there was a comfy bed that I could rest my eyes on
Once there was food that I could feast on at meal times
Once there was a family that cared for me
Once there were clothes that I could wear and they were clean
Once there was a school that I went to, to learn
Now there is a Kommandant who doesn't look after us at all,
Who is very healthy, very wealthy and very, very tall.

Meghan Williamson (12)
Ripon Grammar School, Ripon

The House

Deep in the woods there is a house,
Where no one lives but a field mouse,
Overgrown gardens and dirty sinks,

Now unloved and abandoned,
Just lying there waiting for something to have happened,
No one knows about this dirty old house,
Except for the previous owners and the field mouse,

No one sees this very old house,
Not even forest creatures just the field mouse.

Sam Bland (13)
Ripon Grammar School, Ripon

As You Slipped Away From Me

As you slipped away from me,
Into the life after death.
I wondered,
Why me?
All this pain,
Why me?
Why ruin my life?
Beeeep the line went straight.

You slipped away . . .

Christina Scullion (11)
Ripon Grammar School, Ripon

Life

This means the world to you and me,
Without life there would be nothing,
No colour, no happiness, no sadness.

The world would be a lump of rock, and no more,
Everything that brings us happiness would not exist,
We are life; without us nothing could be the same.

Alice Shanahan (12)
Ripon Grammar School, Ripon

What Matters To Me

What matters to me,
Is my mind, no, memory,
Well not so much memory but memories,
Which without it would be impossible to seize,
What you really love, or like,
Like how to ride a bike,
Or the new bed that you got,
To replace your old cot,
Or the markings on the wall,
To check whether or not you're tall,
Or your first day at school,
And how you thought you were so cool,
With your shirt tucked in and top button done up,
And the drink you brought in your Bob the Builder cup,
That's what matters to me.

What matters to me is memories and holidays,
And how we used to laugh and play,
And have the perfect picnic on the beach,
Or when my mum would have to bleach,
The mud, from my mucky, mucky trousers,
After we'd trekked back to our wooden houses,
And after a long day kayaking on a Scottish loch,
The curtains would finally block,
The light from my now dark bedroom,
And how my time asleep would zoom,
And when I'd wake up from a good night's sleep,
A beam of sun through the curtain would peep,
And I'd look behind the curtain to see what type of day it may be,
And I would see the sun crawling over the horizon, iridescent on the sea,
That's what matters to me.

What matters to me is my old house,
And how I used to live between the Scouse,
And the Manchester lot,
And all the memories I've got,
Of a place called Warrington,
Where I became my mum's second son,
And lived there for 12 years of my life,
And how I got through all the pain and strife,

Of moving to Harrogate,
And losing my best mate,
And my first day at my new school,
And how I thought I really wasn't cool,
With my shirt tucked in,
And top button done up,
And the drink that I brought in my new cup,
That's what matters to me.

What matters to me is memories to come,
And hoping that I will have some,
With my new best mate,
And how the things we do are so great,
Like when we go swimming to the pool,
And how I can think I'm cool,
With my shirt un-tucked and top button undone,
And all the things we can do in the summer sun,
Like mess about with a football,
Until my mum would eventually call,
For me to go back to my house,
That's not between the Scouse,
And the Manchester lot,
So what matters to me are the memories I've got,
That's what matters to me.

Josh Day (13)
Rossett High School, Harrogate

Time

What is time?
Time is neither here nor there
It is unbreakable yet so fragile
It never stops yet never starts
Time is worthless yet so valuable
Time can be your best friend or your worst enemy
What is time?
It's simply awesome.

Joe Porter (13)
Rossett High School, Harrogate

What Matters To Me?

As I gaze into the mirror,
And stare deep into my eyes,
I search through what's inside me,
Most of which, what others can't see.

I steal my make-up bag from my dresser;
I'm the thief and it's my gold,
I start putting my face on,
As if it's some priceless Picasso.

I am now masked.
Now the fake me . . .
Well not so much fake . . .
More just unreal.

My mask protects me,
Almost barricades me
From the outside world, from my own feelings,
After all, my weakness is that I care too much.

It lets me feel nothing, my mask
So that, emotionless
I can carry on with my life
Without being interrupted by feelings.

However my mask feels almost natural now
As if it's melted into my skin
And become part of me,
The unreal me, that is.

Despite this, my mask can be broken down,
Almost destroyed,
With the feeling of trust, loyalty, understanding.
The feeling of having a true friend.

Seeing their smile
And having a tear run down your face
Just from knowing they're happy
From knowing they're alright.

Having someone to look past the outside,
Break through your soul
And gaze in on the sincerity within you,
Even if it takes a while to get there.

So what matters to me?
With a tear in my voice,
I said, 'That's the question.'
Does this deafening silence mean nothing to no one but me?

Lorna Clark (14)
Rossett High School, Harrogate

What Matters To Me

I love football,
You can be tall or small,
It matters to me,
I play it daily.

I think winning is everything,
When I win something,
It should be on the news,
Because I never lose,

People say I'm full of myself,
But as long as I've got my health,
And people don't stare,
Then I don't care.

I really love electricity,
I play on my Nintendo Wii,
I watch television for hours,
'Simpsons, Family Guy, Austin Powers'.

I hope you like this rap,
Now I'm going to take a nap,
It was about what matters to me,
So please don't take the mickey!

Ben Parker (14)
Rossett High School, Harrogate

An Ode To Tea

What really matters to me,
Is something that'll suit my needs,
And soothing painful addictive pleads,
Something that is part of my culture,
And will stay with me in the future,
Something sweet but optionally sour,
And will make all my other needs cower,
Well every day I need tea,
But which tea for which day? We'll see . . .
When I'm down I'll have PG Tips,
Not gulps, just little sips,
To settle my tears,
From falls of peers,
Perhaps peppermint when I've taken ill,
Lie on the sofa and put it on the window sill,
Watch the prancing waves walk up the glass,
Draw a smiley face from the leftover mass,
Feel it smoke into my pipes and beyond,
The feeling of intensity, oh I am fond.
Let's see,
To me,
Green tea,
Is a strange little remedy,
Partners with conspiracy,
For some hallucinations,
For others relaxations,
One thing for sure,
Your energy bill will give you a fright,
For your toilet will be flushed more than twice a night,
Camomile smells like flowering seeds,
But with a sip, it'll taste of weeds,
Say no to coffee, I like my eight hours,
No to green tea, I'm not a relaxer, not baths, just showers,
PG Tips - love the monkey,
But it tastes too modern, too funky.
In my house we're Yorkshire Tea girls,
It turns our hair to curls,
Now one sugar, dash of milk,

Tastes like pure, fresh silk.
On a saucer and my favourite mug,
I'll pass off other teas, with a shrug,
Yorkshire Tea
That matters to me.

Sarah Jane Littlejohn (13)
Rossett High School, Harrogate

What Matters To Me

What matters to me, let's see . . .
Well of course, love!
Not that sweetie pie stuff,
But the type that isn't easy to see,
Like, the love between friends,
Who will be there till the end,
And will always be there for me!

I have many good friends,
They're like angels, Heaven-sent.
And the nicest I'll ever meet.
And when I grow old,
I'll remember when I was told.
'You can always find a friend in me'!

My best friend, she's the best,
Even though she's a pest,
She knows every single thing about me.
Although she never shows it,
She loves me and she knows it.
And *that* is what matters to me.

Nicole Leaver (14)
Rossett High School, Harrogate

The Things That Matter To Me

What matters to you?
Family, friends, pets!
Or the education at school too?
What matters to you?
Health, welfare, chocolate!
Or even the memories too?
What matters to you?
Trust, love or even music!
What else matters to you?

The things that matter to me the most,
Are family, friends, love and the sea's coast,
That's what matters to me.

First off, why family?
They mean so much to me,
No matter what you do,
They'll be there to support you,
They will care and protect you,
As well as cheer you up too.

Now secondly, about friends
They're always there until the end,
They back you up and never give up,
They're crazy, funny and out of the blue, they shout, 'Duck'!
They keep secrets and they're trustworthy,
Sometimes we all talk and never get bored, sat under a birch tree.

Well thirdly, about love,
There's always a pair of turtle doves,
One may be crazy, the other silly,
Another fussy and one that likes chilli,
There's another half for everyone out there,
Always looking, for their life to share.

And finally, the sea's coast,
I adore its breathtaking views the most,
The horizon with the waves and sunset,
Standing on the beach to see this, is the best bet,
The sand on the beach is soft yet rough,
It's what makes a beach a beach, it's the best stuff.

That's what matters to me the most,
Family, friends, love and the sea's coast,
That's what matters to me.

Leif Anderson (13)
Rossett High School, Harrogate

What Matters To Me

What matters to me brings together my life,
Bonding and binding features of my complex lifestyle together.

Music; you hear it, play it, live it, use it, make it, love it.
Sport; you hear it, play it, live it, use it, make it, love it.

But then there are family and friends, you need to keep them closer to help you in dark times.
Then there are my hobbies, you need to keep them close to cheer you up in dark times.

Foods keep me alive and well during what I do through my days.
Drink keeps me alive and well during what I do through my days.

They all make a difference but what matters most is me
A fusion of all those things.

My life together, everything means something.
It makes me.
And that ain't gonna change.
The one and only.
Me.

Joe Hallas (14)
Rossett High School, Harrogate

What Matters To Me

What matters to me,
Is for my friends to be,
Happy and free,
Like the Dead Sea,
But some may disagree . . .

What matters to me,
Is the creation of thee,
That looks out to be,
A retreat,
But some may disagree . . .

What matters to me,
Is the food that we eat,
That we eventually excrete,
Down the ejection seat,
Which is usually in the en suite . . .

What matters to me,
Is my mum and family,
As they are there for me,
But I can't wait for them to be as tall as my knee,
So I can be there for thee . . .

What matters to me,
Is my health degree,
When I go to the doctors they agree,
Whoopee . . .
My life will continue freely.

What matters to me,
Is my memories that spree
Throughout my family tree,
I guarantee . . .
That you will have many to see . . .

That is what matters to me.

Brandon Andrews-Bligh (14)
Rossett High School, Harrogate

That's What Matters To Me

My super best friends,
They're there till the end,
Loving and caring,
Secrets worth sharing,
We smile and we weep,
We sing and we leap,
That's what matters to me.

Walking round town,
Clowning around,
Messing about,
Without a doubt,
Painting my nails,
Reading my emails,
That's what matters to me.

They're always there,
Ready to care,
They help me through,
The rough times too,
Cheer me up when I am blue,
That's my superb family,
That's what matters to me.

My musical passion,
My love for fashion,
Clothes and shoes,
Accessories too,
Doing my bit,
Keeping healthy and fit,
That's what matters to me.

Family and friends,
Music and feelings,
Love and animals,
Faith and trust,
All of these and memories,
That's what matters to me!

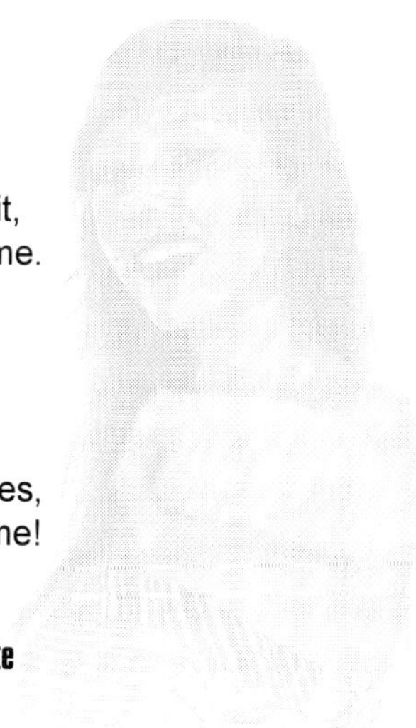

Katie Sandever (13)
Rossett High School, Harrogate

What Matters To Me

I stand in front of my big mirror,
Always after I've eaten my dinner,
I'm scared to look but then I think,
Go on just take a blink.

Every day when I have to wake up,
I can't wait to slap on some make-up,
I hide what I don't want people to see,
I'll never let people see the real me.

All my friends are just so pretty,
And then well, then there's me,
I'm just so different to them,
They're like a perfect gem.

Why do I always look like a mess?
And I never look good in a dress,
Maybe someday I might be,
Somebody's bride-to-be.

Amy White (13)
Rossett High School, Harrogate

Animal Cruelty

It's a harsh time hearing about it,
It's a hard time seeing it,
It's horrible knowing about it,
But what can we do?
They treat them like their lives are nothing.
And like they don't exist.
They are pushed around, abused and wounded
But they can only hope for someone
Who will come and help them live a better life!

Chloe Broom (13)
Rossett High School, Harrogate

What Matters To Me?

What matters to me,
Are my friends and family
And having someone there for me,
When I need them the most.

I spend time with my friends.
We have amazing memories
I'm with them all the time,
And that's what matters to me.

I have my health
Got love,
Got happiness
But that's not all that matters to me.

I care what people think about me,
I care what I look like,
I've got my pets,
And that's what matters to me.

Rachel Garner (13)
Rossett High School, Harrogate

What Matters To Me?

Happiness is what matters to me,
And what makes me happy is unique to me.
Food is something that makes me happy,
The taste of it, the smell of it are what makes me happy.
Football is another thing that keeps me going.
It's fun, fast moving and gets me going.

What makes me happy is more important than anything,
So happiness is the most important thing of all.

Matthew Williamson (14)
Rossett High School, Harrogate

What Matters To Me

Everyone's heart is ticking,
Ticking away as we live,
It ticks in a rhyme,
Ticking through time.

Everyone's hearts are ticking,
They skip in excitement,
Our ticking may go fast,
But it can stop in an instant.

Everyone's hearts are ticking,
We take this for granted,
The ticking in our lives,
Ticking till the end of time.

Without time,
I wouldn't be able to survive,
Different things,
That's why it's crucial to me.

Ben Watson (13)
Rossett High School, Harrogate

What Matters To Me?

Vanity has nothing to do with me,
Now I know it does not concern me.
I think that it has no reason to be.
I think that some are far too proud.
They broadcast who they think they want to be,
I know the things that matter to me.

Are certainly not vanity.

Inequality is our way of life,
Which many will try to strive.
Fools, they know that it does exist,
We must accept this,
This dark abyss,
Of the rest of our lives.

Equality is an illusion
Inequality is our way of life.

Ben Laws (14)
Rossett High School, Harrogate

Happy

What matters to me?
To be honest, I'm not sure,
It could be laughing with my friends,
Getting more and more and more,
But what matters to me?
Should it be deep and meaningful?
Should I be making sure that the inside is beautiful?
Or is it something more? Maybe I can't see it,
Maybe the signs are right in front of me and I just can't see it!
But essentially, if it matters to me, it should matter you,
What matters to me?
Up late, in late, family, Harrogate! Jack Wills, no pills, thanks,
No friends, London, my religion, musk, being happy, equality,
What matters to me?
Well, do I have to pick one?

Sorcha Monaghan (13)
Rossett High School, Harrogate

What Matters To Me

There are a few things that I take for granted,
It's not my fault, but in my mind it's planted,
Like a seed in the earth,
Not much,
But what it's worth,
Could change a life somewhere,
A life where people may not care.
And that care is what I take for nothing,
I don't realise that my mum does the washing,
The cleaning, the cooking, the tidying,
The little things matter to me,
If it's just a smile, or a cup of tea
I'm grateful that I get what I need,
This is what matters to me.

Sarah Elwen (13)
Rossett High School, Harrogate

What Matters To Me?

What matters to me?
There are a lot of things there could be
I mean I'm smart, I'm sporty,
But . . .
What really matters to me,
Are my friends, my family,
Who always do things happily.
I do what they say,
Cos when they go away,
I will well up inside,
And fall into a deep black hole,
With no escape pole.
But my friends and family will never leave,
And that's all that matters to me.

Alex Marks (13)
Rossett High School, Harrogate

Arshavin

There's a player called Arshavin
His first match was against Liverpool
He scored four goals on his debut
Which made him look so cool.

After the match the fans all applauded for Arshavin
For the four goals he smashed past Reina.
The fourth goal was the best
It was such a powerful shot
That Arsene Wenger decided to give him a rest.

Gerrard and Torres were so upset
It made them scream, 'Arshavin's the best'
At the end of the match
Rafa Benitez said, 'Maybe it wasn't such an easy test.'

Haider Ali (14)
St Bede's Catholic Grammar School, Heaton

Equality

Life is time
Time is life
No murders will appear
At the time of night

Love is good
It's our key
I'm friends with them
They're friends with me

Joyful, kindness
Kindness, joy
It doesn't matter
If you're a girl or a boy

Light or darkness
Darkness or light
It makes no difference
If you're black or white

We are all unique.

Mohsin Ali (11)
St Bede's Catholic Grammar School, Heaton

Undercover

U nlikely place for,
N eed of speed,
D angerously good cars,
E verywhere around.
R eventon, Lamborghini
C hanges gear soon
O ut of here.
V eyron soon overtakes,
E very single car, in the
R ace.

Hasan Rasib (13)
St Bede's Catholic Grammar School, Heaton

The Week

T he early mornings make us groan, as the weekend is now just a distant memory and a new week of school starts.
H urrying out of the front door to catch my bus and hoping it doesn't appear.
E very hour feels like a lifetime, as you wait for the last bell to ring, meaning the day is over.

W ednesdays bring joy, as they signify the middle of the week and knowing Friday is near.
E veryone gets giddy on Thursday, as Friday and the weekend are just a short time away.
E xcitement gushes through the school, as the final bell sounds and then you know the weekend has begun.
K ids across the nation wait for the weekend, but as Sunday evening draws closer it is back to early nights and early mornings and the weekday cycle starts again.

Thomas Carpenter (13)
St Bede's Catholic Grammar School, Heaton

Snowboarding

S lippery, steep, scary slopes slither, seemingly,
N ever leave without your clothes,
O r without your board!
W inter weather sprinkles your face,
B y any means stay safe;
O r else . . .
A ccurately, I plummeted,
R apidly
D own the steep slopes
I scream in fear and
N odded to the cameraman filming my
G reat attempt!

Jack I'Anson (12)
St Bede's Catholic Grammar School, Heaton

My House

Though I take it for granted
I have realised that it's good
Because it is better than living in the mud.
It is my house.

I eat in it every day
No one is in the way.
It is my house.

I have my personal space
And I think it has a face.
It is my house.

Jordan Harding (13)
St Bede's Catholic Grammar School, Heaton

Dead Love

The sky falls, the death tolls.
Planets explode, so do our roads.
People bend, the world ends.
The universe rips, here at the apocalypse.

But it's all anonymous, because my wife is right there.
I hold her hand, stroke a lock of hair, 'I love you,' I say,
She responds, 'Goodbye, together forever, and together we die.'

Jacob Lalor (13)
St Bede's Catholic Grammar School, Heaton

Ugly Bully

B ullies are the meanest people around
U niting each other
L iking people who are tough
L iking people who are strong
Y ou don't want to be a bully.

Rhiece McDonagh (11)
St Bede's Catholic Grammar School, Heaton

My Beach Party

At my beach party
What a great day
Lots of smiles and laughter
Hip, hip, hooray.

Fabulous Frankie
Is very funky
Eating all the Jaffa Cakes
Yum, yum, yum.

Next banging Beth
Best friends with Steph
Jumping over the waves
Every time she says

Now superb Steph
Last one left
Laid in her bikini
Drinking a Martini.

And finally there's me
Happy as a bee
Everything was fine
What a good time!

Laura Sugden (11)
South Holderness Technology College, Preston

What Matters To Me?

Sport is important to me,
Especially Hull FC,
Black and white is all the way,
And going to watch them play.

Family and friends are great,
Mainly my best mate,
Her name is Chloe,
We have a laugh together,
Hopefully we will be friends forever.

I love the sun,
It is so much fun,
Going on holiday is the best,
Playing in the pool with my sister
And then having a nice long rest.
Bulgaria was my favourite holiday.
We are going to go back, my mum and dad say.

I like to go spend some dosh,
And to look nice and posh,
Buying clothes from New Look and Topshop,
And buying a new CD which is obviously hip hop.

I also really enjoy horse riding,
When I'm riding along it makes me sing,
Cantering in the fields with the wind in my hair,
But when it comes to falling off, it gives me quite a scare.

Autumn is one of my favourite times of year you see,
I don't know why, but it must be,
Crunching along as you walk in the leaves,
But no sight of any of the bees.

I love to eat sour sweets,
The taste in my mouth is so neat,
Soda bottles are the best,
A lot better than all the rest.

I have four sisters and I love them a lot,
Three of them are triplets, but identical they're not.
Then there's my younger sister, Ellie,
She likes the taste of red jelly,
She can be at times such a little monkey,
But then at others, quite cool and funky.

These were some of the things that matter to me!

Amy Medforth (13)
South Holderness Technology College, Preston

The Four Seasons

Spring
In spring I was a curled up bud,
I wanted to grow, I knew I could!
I began to sprout strong and tall,
I just had to await my lucky call.

Summer
In summer I grew to a tremendous extent,
I was pretty much there, I couldn't pretend.
I had blossomed into a beautiful flower,
Even though there was barely a shower.

Autumn
I grew sad and depressed as I watched my stem fall and die,
I saw the wonderful autumn colours and could only sigh.
I wished I could only be like that,
But all I could do was sit, and so I sat.

Winter
And now it was so cold, I doubted I would blossom tall,
I wanted to be best, better than them all.
I imagined spring, oh praise the mighty then!
I can't wait for it all to happen again.

Schaunagh Clair Gleeson (11)
South Holderness Technology College, Preston

I Want A Bike . . .

I want a bike with a rigid frame,
A beast of a bike which is barely tame,

One that flies past the cars,
A bike with dropped handlebars,

A quick racing bike that cannot be caught,
That can rack up the miles, a rapid onslaught,

Destroy the hills that are marathon long,
Then I'd have thighs like Lance Armstrong,

If only I had multiple gears,
Then I'd have the bike the pelaton fears,

A fast bike that would be great,
Carbon components very lightweight,

Spokes as strong as a powerful ox,
Wheels that creep like a wily fox,

It must be as light as a feather,
A seat made of the finest leather,

A bike that can take any lead,
A bike with a terrifying turn of speed,

World class brakes that grip like a vice,
A swift derailleur what a device,

A nimble bike that's all I need,
A trusty old ten speed,

A red bike so very slick,
The professional rider's personal pick,

Oh no, it doesn't end there,
I can't be seen dead without some Lycra sportswear.

Joseph Dean (13)
South Holderness Technology College, Preston

My Family

Forever I will love my mum
Forever I will love my dad
When I am with them, I am never sad
With them behind me, my life will never be bad.

I love my brother, Alex, even though he can be annoying,
But fun games are all he plays,
I love him in many different ways.

Forever I will love my nanna, I see her every day.
She gives the best hugs in every single way.

Forever I will love my grandad, I love it when he plays his drums,
I get prouder that he's my grandad every day.

I will always love my Uncle Phill, he plays his guitar every day,
I love him in every single way.

My Auntie Vick is awesome, she's always very fashionable,
Of everything she is capable.

My Auntie Ruth came into my life when I was 10,
I've loved her ever since then.

My mum is truly awesome.
I love her so much.
She's got the loving magic touch
Every night we sit and have a cup of tea
And she tells me how much she loves me.

My dad is my athletics coach, he comes with a nice approach.
I love him immensely much
He has got the magic touch.

So on the whole, my family are awesome and important to me
So let's settle down and have a cup of tea.

Megan Grant (11)
South Holderness Technology College, Preston

My Family

My family is just
Like any other
With a mum and
A dad and a
Little brother.

My dad
Is annoying with
His practical jokes.
I've got a big bunch
Of cousins and a load
Of old folks.

I've got a little brother
Who can scream, laugh
And shout!
And can always
Get around you
With his little pout.

I've got an annoying
Brother, but he's as
Caring as my
Mother.

My mum
Is great and
There will never
Be another.

Then there is only
One more left
My big old dog, Zakk, who's an
Almighty pest.

Rebecca Caley (11)
South Holderness Technology College, Preston

Party At The Beach!

Come to the party,
With meee,
Bring your swimsuit,
Or bikini,
Come in the sea,
With meee.
Laughing with friends,
Screaming in the sun.
Build a sandcastle,
With meee,
Chucking that water,
Drenching all my friends.
Fabulous Frankie,
Always needs a hankie,
Her nose bleeds all day,
That's why I stay away.
Loopy Laura,
Loves her Dora,
Does scream if you,
Go to the loo.
Sassy Steph,
Just loves her Beth,
If she gets banging,
She'll never get stopping.
We're travelling home,
We will come back,
Because next time,
We'll do it again.

Bethanie Harrison (11)
South Holderness Technology College, Preston

Friends

Gorgeous Georgia
Generous as anything
Likes playing Care Bears

Outrageous Olivia
She's very loud
And sticks out from a crowd

Silly Steph
Brilliant Beth
Two of my mates

Fabulous Frankie
Is a bit lanky
Addicted to her horses
And likes playing with her own little sources

Loopy Laura
Is so lively
Likes being normal

KitKat Kira
Likes playing kitties
She is so mental

Lively Loren
Is so wacky
Likes playing.

Chelsie Butler (11)
South Holderness Technology College, Preston

My Pets

My pets, I've four all knocking on my door
My dog, Remus likes chewing his toys
My cat, Allie, sometimes scratches my dog
My fish live to just swim around the pool.

Alex Peers (11)
South Holderness Technology College, Preston

Swimming Club

Swimming training,
Swimming galas,
Christmas parties,
With a
Happy elfman!

Swimming training,
Swimming galas,
Messing about,
With friends,
So fun!

Swimming training,
Swimming galas,
Laughing a lot,
Splashing coaches,
They're soaked!

Swimming training,
Swimming galas,
Sprinting lengths,
So tiring,
Training's over!

Bethany Colclough (12)
South Holderness Technology College, Preston

Home

Look at this world and what do you see?
It's just a world to you and me
But closer and it's your home
So don't ruin the ozone
Turn off lights and kill the kettle
Recycle paper and scraps of metal
So now you've looked closer I hope you see
It's more of a home to you and me.

Chloe Leathley (11)
South Holderness Technology College, Preston

Sweets

Sweets, sweets, those tasty treats,
Always there for me to eat.
Becketts, Co-op, they're everywhere,
Liquorice, Randoms and Golden Bears.

Different colours and bursting with flavours,
Luckily sweets don't have behaviours.
Chewy, crunchy, hard and sour
Sweets have that special power.

Mouth-watering, *yum, yum*,
All those sweets, in my tum!
Stars, circles, shapes and sizes,
And all those great surprises.

Sweets can make you go on a high,
They can even make you fly.

Lots of things make sweets great,
And you don't have to use a plate.
If I don't have them, I will whine,
But I love them because they're all mine!

Yippee!!

Louise Heppell (11)
South Holderness Technology College, Preston

Autumn Express

The nights go dark.
And it's hard to park.
The leaves blow away.
And that's what I say.
The big tall trees.
To the buzzing bees.
Red, gold, yellow, brown.
I don't wanna see a frown.

Elize Sherwood (11)
South Holderness Technology College, Preston

Our Teachers

Our teacher is a creature,
Like no other he has a brother,
But he is normal and terribly formal,
The shame he puts on Mr Grame,
Our teacher is quite fat,
His chin looks big with that leopard hat,
Chequered shirt, floral skirt, with cowboy boots and tattooed floats.
With size 54 feet, he's someone you'd hate to meet.
But Mrs Loral is the worst,
She sings songs with Mrs Hirst.
She does science in complete silence,
Mr Jumps has got the mumps,
Mrs Lelly has a big belly,
Mrs Hope likes to jump a rope.

They're all crazy, it makes me hazy,
The worst of all is called Paul,
He's the master, his rules get faster
The list gets bigger
He'll pull the trigger for fun
Oh no, he stole my chocolate bun. Argh!

Leah Fewlass (11)
South Holderness Technology College, Preston

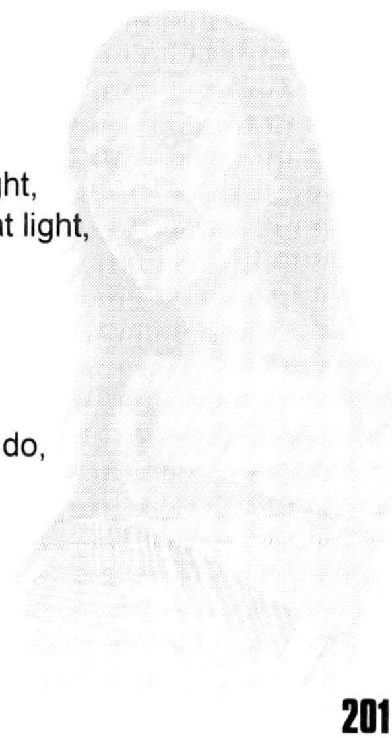

Dreamland

The trusty steed awakens in the blackness of night,
Takes me away to dreamlands so unspeakable at light,
The silky golden mane upon its head,
Dreaming of it all day, you cannot wait for bed.

Family and friends so fantastic too,
They blow you away with dreamy things too,
The things that they say and the things that they do,
They're amazing, do you think so too?

Georgia Bailey (11)
South Holderness Technology College, Preston

My Room, Room, Room

My bed is a roller coaster,
That shoots up and down.
My wardrobe is a haunted house,
With a clown that wears a scary frown.

My room, room, room is a brand new world,
When the moon, moon, moon comes up.

My bed is the ocean,
Which swirls and swishes.
My boxes are coral reef,
Full of multicoloured fish.

My room, room, room is a brand new world,
When the moon, moon, moon comes up.

My room is:
Fairground
Seaside
Footy pitch
Toy shop
My room is whatever I want it to be.

Rosie Jukes (11)
South Holderness Technology College, Preston

Advent

Christmas is near,
So open the door,
And you will find a chocolate in store,
When children's presents
Are whispering secrets.

The countdown is here,
So Santa is near,
The reindeer are as excited as Santa,
For this Christmas to come.

Nakia Brown (11)
South Holderness Technology College, Preston

My Family Poem

I have a sister,
Who is older than me.
She listens to pop and rock,
And likes to drink tea.

I have a younger sister,
Who is bonkers and fun.
She listens to rock music,
And likes to eat a chocolate bun.

I have twin brothers,
Who are funny and loud.
They like to sing on a stage,
And always get a crowd.

I have a mum and dad,
They are no fools.
They will sing with me on Singstar,
They are very cool.

This is a poem about what is special to me,
I love my family as you can see.

Sophie Wood (11)
South Holderness Technology College, Preston

Super School Bus

S houting out the window
C ool kids sitting next to me
H aving fun on the bus, weee!
O ut cruising on the bus not
O range juice has just been splashed on me
L aughing on the bus, yo!

B eing a bit crazy
U nderneath the seat, there's money!
S chool is boring, yo!

James Beck (11)
South Holderness Technology College, Preston

Poetry

The evil side of telly
If you watch a lot of telly
You'll end up looking like a pile of jelly.

Cheese
Give me cheese, give me cheese
Give me cheese, cheese, cheese
Please, please, please.

Pets
The horse gallops in the field
The dog barks at the window
The cat miaows in the mill
The hamster runs around the cage many times
The fish breathes through its gills.

The star
I'm a star, twinkling in the sky
Seeing every passer-by
Oh no, the sun's coming out to play
That's enough twinkling for one day.

Jess Green (11)
South Holderness Technology College, Preston

Judo

My favourite sport is judo
It makes you think like a game of Cluedo
You work so hard you nearly faint
Your face goes red like a bucket of paint
We wear belts from red to black
In the corner of the room there are trophies on a rack
There are lots of pictures placed upon the walls
At the beginning of the lesson, we play with footballs
In judo, we always do sweeps
When we get thrown, we end up in heaps.

Scott Taylor (11)
South Holderness Technology College, Preston

What Matters To Me

Chocolate, chocolate, it's so cool,
Chocolate, chocolate makes me drool,
Chocolate I could eat all day,
With chocolate I get carried away.

But time to get back to Earth you see,
Time to get back to my family,
I have a mum who is the best,
Wouldn't change her for the rest.

Friends you need on your side,
When difficulties should arise,
Throughout your life and at school,
Having them is all so cool.

My future is important to me,
I hope it's as easy as 1, 2, 3,
Working hard will be a slog,
But it will be worth it with a job.

And that is what matters to me!

Jordanne-Rose Rodgers (11)
South Holderness Technology College, Preston

Chelsea AFC

Chelsea, good at football
Chelsea, very fast
Chelsea, have good players
Chelsea, have a lot of fans

Chelsea, got a mean manager
Waiting for the players
Sitting in my seat
Looking out for cards
Referees shouting, 'Offside!'
Goal!

Alex Wellburn (11)
South Holderness Technology College, Preston

Cricket

Bowling a fast ball
Hitting it for miles ya'll
Got to the boundary
Went for 4 not 3
I caught it, he's out
No hanging about
Putting my pads on
Aah, my helmet's gone
Got to find it
But my bag's a right pit
My whites are dirty
But it's five thirty
That Corkey's right hard
I need a get well card
Yes we won
My head weighs a ton
I'm off home
To dream of Lords, not Rome.

Alice Johnson (12)
South Holderness Technology College, Preston

Things That Matter To Me

Thoroughbreds canter and gallop with glee.
Arabians prance at the sight of the sea.
A brave hacking horse stands tall and proud.
Show horses canter without making a sound.
A little foal about to be lay
Shetland ponies munching on hay.
Warmbloods can jump as high as a house
Riding school ponies are as quiet as a mouse.
I have a pony better than all of these
I love him more than you'd ever believe
Nothing compares to my pony and me!

Evie Newsom (11)
South Holderness Technology College, Preston

Football

Football, football, score a goal
I guess this match I'm on a roll

Win or lose is still the same to me
Let's just hope I don't need a wee.

Oh no I forgot today's the match
I guess I have to play catch

Kick a ball up high
Maybe it will learn to fly

'Goal, goal!' goes the crowd
They have gone so wild

Score, score, there will be a big roar
'Pass, pass!' goes the player on the grass
Save, save, as the crowd wave

Football, football, what a game.

Luke Ollett (12)
South Holderness Technology College, Preston

My Friends

Even if I'm happy
Or even if I'm sad
All my friends are there for me
To make me feel more glad.

I go with them to dancing
I go with them to sing
If they have a problem
It's me they give a ring.

Without them my life is boring
I need them by my side
They know my biggest secrets
In them, I can confide.

Chloe Whitehead (13)
South Holderness Technology College, Preston

My Pet Rat!

My pet's name was Reggie the rat.
People made me cry because I had him.
He knew when it was bedtime.
He was the best pet ever.
Died a day before Christmas.
Had a big lump on his leg.
Nobody knew he was dead.
All except me.
He was in the same place all night.
When we had takeaway he went to the cage ready to eat.
He had a bed, he ate it up.
When we put him in a ball, he wouldn't move.
I guess he was more spoilt than me.
He was black and white.
We had him for a year or something.
He was so cute I wish I had him now.

Georgia Hogarth (11)
South Holderness Technology College, Preston

Pain Barrier

Blood and sweat
Before we all properly
Met!

Throughout the game
We all experience
Pain!

Dumped in mud
Pouring lots of
Blood!

Why be king
When you're a
Holderness Viking?

Connor Dutton (13)
South Holderness Technology College, Preston

The Bus!

Rocking the bus yeah!
The driver isn't cool.
Chanting and screaming
Says the oldest in
The school.

Cool kids sit at the back
Some people give them a
Whack, ooh, that's gonna hurt.

I have some friends
Isaac and Miles are cool.
My brother, Alex, isn't a drool.
Hey soul sister beating
In my ear, the song is
Ace, turning it off is a
Disgrace.

Jack Johnson (11)
South Holderness Technology College, Preston

The Wild

Birds ready to fly
Right up in the sky
Trees all around me
Swarming all over
Deer fighting for mates
Calves playing about

Sheep climbing hills
Farmers driving quads
People walking dogs
The wind blowing
Everything now
The wilderness
A dream come true.

Ewan Maltby (11)
South Holderness Technology College, Preston

The Game

Chocolate oh chocolate
So tasty and nice
It gives me strength
To play the game
Oh the pointless game
With no thrills or
Frights.

Charlie's my name
And fame is my
Game.

Number 1 in the world
Owning the nation
Like a twirl, got
To go, COD awaits
Me.

Charlie Thornton (13)
South Holderness Technology College, Preston

My Family

My mum, sister, brother and dad,
What possibly could go bad?
My mum is the best mum in the world,
With her hair in beautiful curls,
My dad is funny and kind,
And mostly never changes his mind.
My brother is frantically weird,
He's lucky he doesn't have a beard.
My baby sister most of all.
Cute and stumbles,
But never grumbles, especially at food time.
That's it, my fantastic family.
Then there's me!

Aiesha Khan (11)
South Holderness Technology College, Preston

Spaceship

Spaceship was big,
Spaceship was tall,
It had a pig,
That was small.

It flew across space,
And then I saw,
It had no face,
But just one floor.

It hit the sun
Super fast,
They saw the nun
They closed their eyes . . . *blast*

They blew up.

Zak Gardner (11)
South Holderness Technology College, Preston

The First Ever Goal I Scored For My Team

It was the last game of the season,
My mum said, 'You have to score.'
So I warmed up, started the game and before you know it
There is was, a wonder strike.
What a goal! I did it!
He shoots, he scores, back of the net,
Chipped right over the keeper's head.
Goals galore, he scored another in a matter of time,
His friend also on the double four-nil
Second game not as good,
No goals again, just a loss.
What a game,
Last match, how did he do it?
Just excellent encouragement of his mum.

Tommy Weightman (11)
South Holderness Technology College, Preston

Doctor Who

First comes the 10th Doctor
Then the Daleks and the Cyber Men
Second comes the assistant, Rose Tyler
Third comes both Daleks and Cyber Men
Fourth comes Martha
Fifth, Judoon
Sixth comes Donna, a right gob
Seventh, Davoros looks like my Uncle Paul
Eighth the 11th Doctor and Amy Pond
And last but not least
Ninth the end of the episode 'til Christmas
Noooooooooooooo
'Yes!'
Who said that?

Cameron Stell (11)
South Holderness Technology College, Preston

My Sister

My sister wakes in the morning,
And spreads her bad breath,
She leaves to go to school,
And my mum cleans her mess.

She is really annoying,
I have to live with it.
She makes a lot of noise.
She doesn't wake from her pit.

She eats the last slice of pizza,
She doesn't really share,
She parties too much,
But in the end she's my sister
And I love her very much.

Connor Goode (11)
South Holderness Technology College, Preston

Me And My Pets

My dog is a little cutie,
He is a little loopy.
My dog has a twin,
Who is a little dim

I have eight fish,
And they live in a dish.
I'd like to make a wish
To have more fish.

I have eight rabbits,
They all have bad habits.
My rabbits are black and grey,
And they play in the hay.

Chloe Dearing (11)
South Holderness Technology College, Preston

Baking And Cooking Away

To mix together an unpromising collection,
Of ingredients and things,
And have them emerge as a truly delicious creation,
Makes me want to sing!

No wonder it is a mystery,
As soon as they enter the oven,
They become a tasty recipe.
As it enters my mouth, I'm in Heaven!

The making may be a bit messy,
And I might get told off a tad,
But it keeps me busy, plus it's tasty,
But when they put it in their mouths, they really are glad.

Morgan Beckitt (12)
South Holderness Technology College, Preston

Computers - My Favourite Thing

Computers are the thing for me,
Without them I wonder . . .
Hmmm, where would we be?
They play a huge part in my life,
And to not have them now
Would cause trouble and strife.

Games, websites, printers and ink
A world without them . . .
Jeez I couldn't think.
I dream about them all the time,
And it's full stop,
The end of my rhyme.

Bradley Steele (11)
South Holderness Technology College, Preston

My Name Is Joe

My name is Joe
Yeah, I ain't a pro.

Never say no
Always takin' home
My sister and my phone
Everywhere I go.

I'm always looking bold
Send me a new tone

Joe just wants to go
Oh just let me go
Eventually get to go.

Joe Taylor (11)
South Holderness Technology College, Preston

The Beginning Of Life

From the security of a mother's womb,
Quietly the baby lays,
Enclosed safely in a compact home,
Preparing for the time ahead
Only accepting the goodness its mother provides,
Kicking a beat to let her know it's there,
Each day becoming stronger and stronger,
Waiting to arrive for all to see,
Bursting into the open and accepting the challenges of life and learning,
The still silence has been broken,
Lay quietly now little one,
Don't be afraid, life has just begun.

Megan Sison (12)
South Holderness Technology College, Preston

The Important Things In Life

I will always remember the 23rd July as this was the day my brother was born.
I waited in the room with my gran for the news to arrive.
So patiently I sat as the clock ticked by.
Why oh why did it have to be today?
I had planned to go swimming that very same day.
But this was much more exciting,
I had waited for this day for nearly nine months.
I never thought he would be here, but now the time is getting so near.
I sat and had those silly thoughts of swimming trips.
Suddenly I realised that having my brother by my side
is the most precious and important thing of all.

Jack Black (11)
South Holderness Technology College, Preston

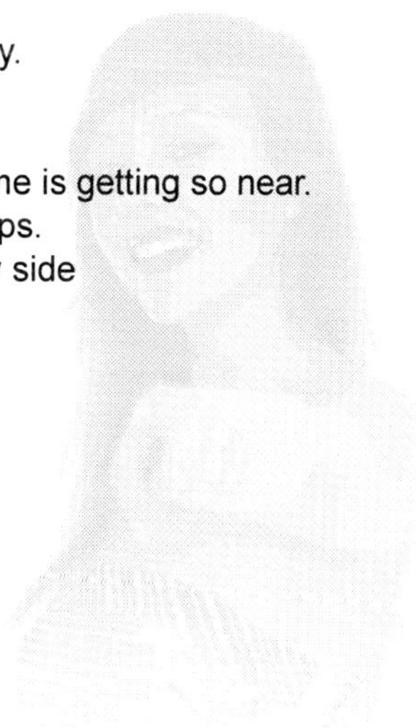

Sport - Me

My name is Ryan
Some people call me Bryan
I'm into cricket
Especially when I get a wicket

Another thing is that I'm into rugby
And I really think that all people should be.

I also like Liverpool
I think that they rule
We talk about them at school
One day I want a house with a swimming pool
That would be really cool.

Ryan Oliver (13)
South Holderness Technology College, Preston

Hull Fair Rap

H aving fun at the best fair called Hull fair
U p the roller coaster, going down yo'll!
L ove in the love mirror, banging yeah mate
L osing money, parents spending money.

F riday, dat's when it starts, Hull fair rules, yeah
A ll the people getting rowdy, banging
I n the ghost train, ghosts all over da place
R unning around yeah, eating all sorts

It's a bit dear but I can wait
'Til next year, yeah hey yo'll.

Christopher Shepherdson (11)
South Holderness Technology College, Preston

On The Bus

Get to the bus at 8 o'clock

S chool nerds sitting at the front
C ool kids sitting at the back listening to music
H ot lasses sitting next to me
O h my gosh going to school
O nly cool teachers are Mr Ladbory, Mr Elvin
L aughing with my mates, not when they pick on little kids.

B ack on the bus on my way home
U niverse playing my music
S chool hasn't been good, yeahhh.

George Williams (12)
South Holderness Technology College, Preston

About Me

Charlie is my name, drama is my game, I like to act and sing and joy to people bring.
At home I like my food, but when I'm in a mood, I argue with my brother 'n' get told off by my mother.
I chill out with my mates around the park gates, but when it gets dark, Dad picks me up from the park.
At night I surf the net looking for the coolest gear, Topman, River Island, but Primark seems more near.
My iPod is my treasure, music is my pleasure, the tracks I like to play I could listen to all day.

Charlie Metcalf (11)
South Holderness Technology College, Preston

Football

Football is so great,
Football is so fast,
Sitting in your seat,
Waiting for the players.

Looking out for cards,
Listening out for people.
Seeing your favourite players,
Looking on the pitch.

Football is so great!

Jai Marrazza (11)
South Holderness Technology College, Preston

Cheese

I tried to fight the urge to eat
But had to taste that cheddar treat.
I had nightmares when I went to bed
I dreamt of a giant otter head.

In the morning I ate cheese.
After that came a massive breeze.
I got blown away in the storm
And I ended up in a big bowl of cheese and corn.

Cheese is what matters to me!

Benjamin Wharton (11)
South Holderness Technology College, Preston

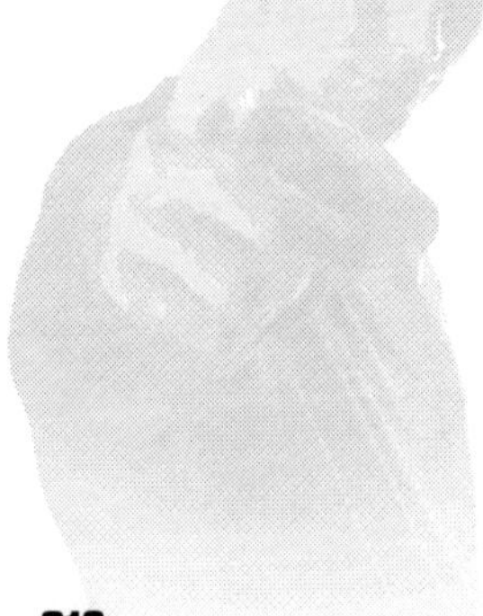

My Cats

My kitten,
He is very smitten,
He is called Georgy,
He is very podgy.

My cat, Alan
He drinks water gallon by gallon,
Alan hates George, cos he always jumps on him.

It's kinda funny until Alan flips out
So George jumps in the bath with fright!

Olivia Jackson (11)
South Holderness Technology College, Preston

My Old Dog, Lucy!

Lucy was a black and tanned Rottweiler.
She was only 3 years old.

Hugs, Lucy always loved her hug any time of the day.
She also had hugs with my rabbit called Peter.

Came in my swimming pool with me if she was hot!

She died of cancer.
She had a big lump on her belly.
My rabbit died on the same day.

Stephanie Poppleton (11)
South Holderness Technology College, Preston

The Roller Coaster

The roller coaster
Is rides of wonder
Everyone loves it
They're having so much fun

From the amount of people
This is the most famous ride
The steepest all around, yeah,
The ride is the world's best ride, yeah.

Jacob Boynton (11)
South Holderness Technology College, Preston

My Life

School doesn't really matter to me
Only swimming, music and PE
Now let me tell you what's really epic:
My friends, mobile and don't you forget it!
My initials are CDP;
Things are bound to go wrong with me,
Like art, science and DT
This is CP out!

Callum Pattrick (13)
South Holderness Technology College, Preston

Big Dogs

Great Danes are tall and thin,
Labradors eat from a bin,
Greyhounds are fast,
St Bernards are vast,
Boxers are awesome,
But Alsations are more fun.

Lauren Baker (13)
South Holderness Technology College, Preston

I Like DVDs

If I'm in a mood, or I'm feeling down,
My DVD player always brings me around.
I watch films like Avatar and 2012.
They make me feel really good about myself.
I think they are great, I think they are funny,
Like the 51st State and World of Bugs Bunny.
Sometimes I think, where would I be
If I couldn't sit down and watch a DVD?

Josh Vickers (13)
South Holderness Technology College, Preston

Marmalade

I have a cat called Marmalade.
He is ginger and furry and loves a good cuddle.
He has great big eyes and long white whiskers.
His favourite food is salmon and tuna.
He is really lazy with a great big smile.
He has two friends that are called Charlie 1 and Charlie 2, which he likes to visit.
I think my cat, Marmalade, is the best cat in the world!

Hannah Hedges (11)
South Holderness Technology College, Preston

Bus Ride

Chatting to friends on the bus
I look outside to see fields of grass
Then suddenly a girl pops up behind me
Shaking with fright
I listen to my iPod just to chill out with cool music.

Ryan Durrant (11)
South Holderness Technology College, Preston

Animals

As the dog woofs, the cat miaows and the horse neighs
A big smile appears on my face
As the little bird cheeps and the guinea pig squeaks
I see the birds open their beaks
Animals have many positives like being soft and cute
But certain animals have a negative
Because we have to pick up their poo
I think we all love at least one animal, whether it's big or small
But to be honest, I think I love them all!

Anna Sugden (11)
South Holderness Technology College, Preston

I Have A Rabbit

I have a rabbit,
Not very brave, not very big.
He might give a bite,
If you give him a fright,
Black and white and a big massive stripe,
Down his back is the stripe,
Dots on back, left and right.
Once I walked with my rabbit,
He also is a great big muppet.

Nathan Lammiman (12)
South Holderness Technology College, Preston

As The Days Turn Grey!

As the days turn grey
My soul is left astray.

As the days turn grey
I feel like I'm fading away.

As the days turn grey
There is now someone to put my mind abay.

Becky Martin (11)
South Holderness Technology College, Preston

Rugby

R ugby is good
U se your strength
G ood players score tries
B oys need to tackle
Y ou will like it.

Jordan Griffiths (11)
South Holderness Technology College, Preston

Young Writers Information

We hope you have enjoyed reading this book - and that you will continue to enjoy it in the coming years.

If you like reading and writing poetry drop us a line, or give us a call, and we'll send you a free information pack.

Alternatively if you would like to order further copies of this book or any of our other titles, then please give us a call or log onto our website at www.youngwriters.co.uk

Young Writers Information
Remus House
Coltsfoot Drive
Peterborough
PE2 9BF
(01733) 890066